My Friend,

B O B B Y

Best wishes,
James Martin

My Friend, **BOBBY**

by
James Martin

BOOK PUBLISHERS

ONE CRANBOURNE ROAD, LONDON N10 2BT

Copyright © James Martin

First published in 1989 by
Arthur James Limited
One Cranbourne Road, London N10 2BT

British Library Cataloguing in Publication Data
Martin, James, 1921 –
My Friend, Bobby.
1. Christian life
I. Title
248.4

ISBN 0-85305-304-9

No part of this book may be reproduced in any
manner whatsoever without the written permission
of the publishers except for brief quotations embodied
in critical articles or reviews.

Typeset by Christel Ivo, London

Printed by The Guernsey Press Co. Ltd,
Guernsey, Channel Islands

Dedication

MY FRIEND, BOBBY

is dedicated to

my grandchildren, Martin, Alison and Gordon
and to Kenneth Ross
and all the children he represents
(in High Carntyne Church, Glasgow,
and Broomknoll Church, Airdrie, particularly)
who through the years appeared to enjoy my
tales of Bobby

Illustrations by
James Simpson
who came to know Bobby well through these talks

Cover by
The Creative House, Saffron Walden, Essex

The Reverend James Martin, MA, BD, DD

was born in Motherwell, Scotland, and trained at Glasgow University. Awarded Gold Medals in Hebrew and Church History, he graduated Master of Arts and Bachelor of Divinity. In 1983 his University conferred upon him the honorary degree of Doctor of Divinity.

After serving in Newmilns West Parish in Ayrshire, he exercised a notable ministry for thirty-three years in the High Carntyne Parish, Glasgow. In retirement he continues his service as a hospital chaplain and as an industrial chaplain.

Well-known in Scotland as a radio and television broadcaster, he has also written

Did Jesus rise from the dead?	(Lutterworth)
The Reliability of the Gospels	(Hodder & Stoughton)
Letters of Caiaphas to Annas	Bles
Suffering Man, Loving God	Saint Andrew Press
Listening to the Bible	Saint Andrew Press
People in the Jesus story	Saint Andrew Press
*The Road to the Aisle	Saint Andrew Press
*A Plain Man in the Holy Land	Saint Andrew Press
*William Barclay: A Personal Memoir	Saint Andrew Press

*still in print

Involved in sport all his life, he still trains, as he has done for many years, with Motherwell Football Club.

Dr Martin is married, has two daughters and three grandchildren

MY FRIEND BOBBY

A Foreword by Ronald Barclay

It would be difficult to find a more suitable person than Jim Martin to have written this book. He is a father and grandfather, well accustomed to the ways of children, a retired minister of the Church of Scotland with many years of service to the Church behind him. He has a distinguished record as a scholar, has written a biography of my father, Dr. William Barclay, and yet he is known to most people as a man of the people and a skilful, down-to-earth communicator. The description of Bobby's excapades stems from a deep understanding of human nature and, young and old, we can all learn from these stories. Preachers in search of children's addresses, parents looking for a different story book for their children, the reader looking for stimulating and meaningful material, those who want to know more about life, all will find something in this book for them. The humour, the communication of the message, the deceptive simplicity of the style, the sudden flashes of insight into an eternal truth, the way in which basic faith is communicated in immediately intelligible terms, those are the factors which make this book different.

We all know Bobby. He is portrayed in a way which is so true to life that we feel we have met him before. And that might just lead us to the heart of this book. You will have a lot of fun reading about Bobby, but every now and again you might just suddenly realise that we don't just know Bobby. We are Bobby! There is a little bit of Bobby in all of us.

Read on and enjoy Bobby and all that he gets up to, but remember, it could have been you!

Contents

	Page
Bobby's bad start *(First Sunday of the Year)*	11
Bobby and the Christmas cards *(Sunday after Epiphany)*	13
Bobby quarrels with his best friend	14
Bobby learns to whistle	16
Bobby sticks up for the minister	18
Bobby has time trouble	19
Bobby and his Valentine	21
Bobby wins the race	23
Bobby and the thunderstorm	25
Bobby has tummy-ache	27
Bobby never gives up	29
Bobby's birthday	31
Bobby and a famous picture *(Passion Sunday)*	33
Bobby and the donkey *(Palm Sunday)*	34
Bobby likes surprises *(Easter Sunday)*	36
Bobby loves Easter *(Low Sunday)*	38
Bobby and Mr Nobody	39
Bobby's present to Dad	42
Bobby and his Mum *(Mothering Sunday)*	44
Bobby finds Jesus at the seaside	46
Bobby loses the power of his legs	48
Bobby jumps over the house	50
Bobby has a 'shares' problem	51
Bobby runs away from home	53
Bobby 'stumps' his friends	55
Bobby blames God	57
Bobby yields to temptation	59
Bobby gets his Wellingtons wet	60
Bobby takes the plunge	64
Bobby likes 'the holidays'	66
When Bobby started school	68
Bobby is disappointed with school	69

	Page
Bobby has a 'test'	71
Bobby and the school photograph	73
Bobby has chicken-pox	75
Bobby touches 'wet paint'	76
Bobby is important	78
Bobby is never afraid if Dad is there	80
Bobby wants a bigger Bible *(Bible Sunday)*	81
Bobby falls out of bed	83
Bobby's dirty hands	86
Bobby and the blackbird's nest	88
Bobby and a misunderstanding	91
Bobby visits a new baby	93
Bobby's pocket	94
Bobby thinks that Susan doesn't count	96
Bobby finds a riddle	97
Bobby makes a snowman	99
Bobby gives Santa Claus a kiss	102
Bobby and the toy Santa	104
Bobby likes the tinsel on the Christmas tree	107
Bobby and the free gift shop *(Christmas Sunday)*	109

First Sunday of the Year

BOBBY'S BAD START

It was just before school closed for the Christmas holidays. Mum woke Bobby up at his usual time but he just did not feel like getting up. He was, in fact, very tired. He thought to himself, "There's really plenty of time. I'll just close my eyes and rest for a minute or two before I get up."

Bobby closed his eyes, laid his head on the pillow and . . . I think you will have already guessed what happened next. Yes, he fell fast asleep again and did not wake up until his mother suddenly realised that everything was quiet in Bobby's bedroom! She came up to see what was wrong.

"Bobby," she shouted, "Bobby, you'll be late for school. Get up at once. You're away behind time."

Bobby jumped out of bed right away. He washed his face, flung on his clothes as quickly as he could, gulped down his breakfast in record time, brushed his teeth like lightning and dashed off to school. Knowing that he did not have much time, he started to run as soon as he was outside and he ran all the way to school.

It was no use. He just could not make up the time he had lost. When he reached the school, he found that the children were already in their classes. Bobby kept on running, right into the school, along the corridor and into his classroom.

"Well, Bobby," his teacher asked, "what does this mean?"

"Please, Miss," Bobby gasped, out of breath, "Please

Miss, I am late." (I think Bobby's teacher already knew that.)

"Yes, Bobby," replied teacher, "you *are* late but you *know* that you should not be late for school. You should have run all the way."

"But I did run all the way," protested Bobby.

"Well, then," teacher said, "I am afraid you were not running fast enough."

"I ran my very fastest," Bobby replied. "The trouble was that I did not start soon enough."

That is often the trouble with many of us over lots of things. We run our fastest once we start, but so often we do not start as soon as we could, and should. If we are to do our best in anything, we *must* begin as early as possible.

If, for example, we are playing in a football match or a hockey match or a tennis match and we do not really start trying until halfway through, then we are letting ourselves and the side down.

To make the best use of this New Year in the service of Jesus, start doing your best for him *right away*.

Sunday after Epiphany

BOBBY AND THE CHRISTMAS CARDS

Bobby was very sad when the Christmas season came to an end and it was time to put away all the Christmas decorations. He would have liked to leave them up in his house for ever, because they were so lovely and bright. But Mum was quite firm. "Tonight is Twelfth Night," she said, "and that is when *all* Christmas decorations *must* be put away."

Bobby was sorry about this and so was his little sister, Susan. They were expecially sorry to see the Christmas tree stripped of its fairy lights, its tinsel and all the other bright things on it that had made it, Bobby was sure, the finest Christmas tree in the whole neighbourhood. But soon the tree was bare and ready to be taken outside and collected later with the other refuse.

The other decorations were taken down and packed away with the tree decorations to await next Christmas. Only the Christmas cards were left, and Mum started to take them down too.

"Mum," said Bobby, "can I have some Christmas cards to keep to play with?"

"Could I have some, too?" piped up Susan.

Mum gave them each a pile of cards, making sure that there was the same number of cards in each bundle. She did not want them to start quarrelling, as they sometimes did, about who had been given the better share. But they did, I am afraid, start to quarrel.

"I've got nicer cards than you," said Bobby.

"No, you haven't. *I've* got nicer cards," Susan protested.

They were sitting on the carpet with their cards beside them, and Bobby picked up one and said, "Look what's on my side, a lovely robin redbreast."

"But see what's on my side," Susan replied, "I have a beautiful church. That's even better."

"That's nothing," Bobby shouted, "I've got the three wise men."

Susan looked glum for a moment and then, as she turned over the next card, her face broke into a smile. "Look at this," she said, "I've got Jesus on my side. That's the best of all."

Bobby knew when he was beaten, and did not argue any more!

Susan was right. It *is* 'best of all' to have Jesus on your side. Decide to let him be there because that is where he wants to be!

BOBBY QUARRELS WITH HIS BEST FRIEND

I expect you have a best friend. I don't mean a sweetheart (although perhaps you have one of those, too). I mean a very special chum. Most boys and girls have one and so does Bobby. Bobby's best friend is called Jimmy and they are very, very good friends indeed.

Sometimes, however, even the best of friends quarrel

(this happens, sadly, with grown-up people too). What is even sadder is that the cause of the argument is often nothing that is very important.

I am sorry to have to tell you that is just what happened one day between Bobby and Jimmy. What it was all about I can't tell you—probably nothing very much. But they had a big, big quarrel and it left Bobby very angry indeed. In fact he was so angry that he decided to write a letter to Jimmy telling him their friendship was at an end. That shows just how angry Bobby was, for it was not long since he had learned to write, and writing a letter was hard work for him. But he was so upset that he just had to write and let Jimmy know that he was not friends with him any more. So Bobby found a pencil and some paper and this is what he wrote:

Dear Jimmy,

I am very angry with you. I am finished with you. I will never play with you again.

>   *love*
>   *Bobby*

Wasn't that a strange way to end such a letter? Bobby did not mean that part, of course. He really meant the rest of the letter, but he did not really mean the 'love' bit. He just thought that was the way all letters ended and so he put it in as a matter of course.

When the Bible tells us that God loves us, we are meant to take that seriously because it is true. God loves us, everyone of us, all the time. Jesus has made that plain. It is the 'good news'.

By the way, Bobby's quarrel with Jimmy did not last very long, you will be glad to know. They were soon firm friends again.

BOBBY LEARNS TO WHISTLE

Bobby can whistle now, yes, *really* whistle! He has been trying to learn how to do it for the last few weeks but did not find it easy. Did you find it easy to learn to whistle?

Bobby was desperately keen to be able to whistle but for a time he thought he was never going to manage it. Every moment he had to spare, you might have seen him standing with his lips pursed and blowing for all he was worth. But no matter how often he tried or how hard he blew, no whistle every came out — until one day when he did produce the faintest little 'peep'. The hardest part was over now and Bobby quickly became better and better at whistling and, in fact, he is now very good at it.

Bobby is very proud of being a good whistler and that is what made him brave enough to speak to the minister the way he did the other day.

Bobby was walking along the street when he saw the minister coming towards him. Bobby not only *saw* the minister! He *heard* him too! But, oh dear, the minister's whistling was not good whistling at all, and that is what caused Bobby to say what he did. "I can whistle, too," said Bobby. "Can you?" said the minister. "Yes," said Bobby. "And I can whistle better than you." "Can you?" said the minister again. "Let me hear you then." So Bobby drew in his breath, puffed out his cheeks and began to whistle his very best whistling.

When he was finished, the minister said to him: "Yes, that is very good whistling indeed, but I think I can beat it." So the minister drew in his breath, puffed out his cheeks and began to whistle. What a surprise Bobby received, for the minister's whistling was easily the best that Bobby had ever heard.

"Now," said the minister when he had finished, "do you think that I beat you?" "Oh yes," replied Bobby, "you are a much better whistler than I am. But when you can whistle like that, why did you whistle the way you did?"

The minister beat Bobby in their whistling competition, but Bobby certainly gave the minister something to think about as he went on his way. Why, indeed, he asked himself, had he been content to whistle badly when he was able to whistle so well?

Do *we* always do our best? Or are we sometimes content, like Bobby's minister, to do a thing badly when we could, if we tried, do it a great deal better?

Do we always do our best for Jesus? After all, he gave his very best for us.

BOBBY STICKS UP FOR THE MINISTER

Bobby is good friends with his minister. The minister likes Bobby and Bobby likes him. But the minister was a bit upset one day when he was walking along a side street in his parish and he came upon Bobby fighting with one of his friends. There they were, rolling about on the pavement, wrestling with each other, going at it hammer and tongs.

The minister was not going to walk past and leave them fighting each other like that. He wanted to try and make them friends again. So he went over to where they were and said, "Come on now. I'm not going to have you fighting each other. Stop it at once and get to your feet."

As he said that, he grabbed hold of them, one in each hand, separated them and hauled them up. They kept glaring at each other but, with the minister there and standing between them, they just could not continue their fight.

"Now," said the minister, "what's the meaning of this? I know that you are friends, so why are you fighting?"

Bobby was the first to speak. What he said surprised the minister.

"It was because of you," Bobby said. "I wanted to stick up for you."

"Because of me?" the minister asked. "What do you mean?"

"Well," Bobby went on, "he said you didn't have the brains of a hen and I said that you had."

It may have been a rather strange way to do it, and a rather strange way to express it, but Bobby really *was* sticking up for his minister. He was being as loyal to him as he knew how.

To be loyal to what is good and true and to stick up for it; to be loyal to the people we love and who love us, and to stick up for them is that lovely.

To be loyal to Jesus and to stick up for him is best of all, even when it causes us difficulty or pain. After all, we could say that, in one sense, Jesus was sticking up for us when he allowed wicked men to put him to death on a cross.

BOBBY HAS TIME TROUBLE

Bobby has been having 'time' trouble and has had it badly. He has again been finding it an effort to get to school in time in the morning. The week before last Bobby was late for school on Wednesday, Thursday and Friday. If there had been any school on Saturday, Bobby would probably have been late then, too!

Bobby was very worried about his lateness. He didn't worry on Saturdays, but as soon as he woke up on Sunday morning, Bobby began to worry again. The teacher had said to him on Friday, "Bobby, I am very displeased with you for coming to school late all these mornings. If you are not in time for school on Monday, I will be very, very angry."

On Sunday morning then, Bobby began to worry about Monday morning. "It will be awful," said Bobby to himself, "if I am late again tomorrow. I do hope I manage to get there in time." He was still worrying when he went to church. At times he was worrying so much that he was not paying much attention to the service. But all of a sudden he sat up straight and began to listen as hard as he was able. For this is what the minister was saying: "If any of you are in trouble, ask God to help you. If something is worrying you, pray to God about it."

Bobby said to himself, "That's me. I will ask God to help me to be in time for school tomorrow." All the way home from church he thought about it and, when he got there, he said to his mum: "Mum, when I say my prayers tonight, I am going to ask God to help me be in time for school tomorrow."

"A good idea," Mum replied. So that night when Bobby was saying his prayers, he said, "and please, God, help me to be in time for school tomorrow so that I won't be late again."

The next morning Bobby got out of bed as soon as Mum called him and he wasted less time than usual putting on his clothes, washing his face, taking his breakfast and getting ready for school. He set out for school in plenty of time. Bobby knew that he was in good time and so, when he came upon workmen tarring the road just a short distance from the school, he stopped to watch—and became so interested that he forgot all about the time. The next thing he knew, the school bell started to ring. That meant he had only two minutes to get into the playground or he would be late again. He took to his heels as fast as he could and, as he ran, he repeated his prayer of the night before, "Please, God, help me to be in time."

Bobby arrived at the school gate just as the bell stopped

ringing. He was running so fast that he tripped and fell headlong through the gate right at the feet of his teacher. It felt as if someone had given him a great big push in the back.

"Well, Bobby", she said, "you're in time this morning, but only just. Another second and you would have been late."

When Bobby arrived home at lunch-time, Mum said right away: "Bobby, were you in time for school today?"

"Yes, Mum," replied Bobby, "just. But if God hadn't given me a push, I would never have managed it."

Maybe God does 'push' us on sometimes. We *all* need that. He knows too just *when* we need it!

BOBBY AND HIS VALENTINE

"Mum," said Bobby one day, right out of the blue, "what is a Valentine?"

It was a week or two before St Valentine's Day, which is on February 14 each year. Bobby had seen a shop window full of cards and a notice which said, "Get your Valentine here."

"A Valentine," Mum told him, "is a message, usually in verse, that a boy or a girl sends on St Valentine's Day to someone they love—but they do not tell them *who* has sent it. It's a secret."

"I love you, Mum," said Bobby, "so could I send *you* a Valentine?"

"No, Bobby," Mum replied, "boys don't usually send Valentines to their mothers. They send them to someone else they're very fond of."

"I'm very fond of the Queen, even though I've never met her," said Bobby. "Could I send a Valentine to *her*?"

"I suppose so," said Mum. "You can either buy a card, if you've any money, or make one up yourself."

"I'll make up my own," said Bobby. Mum thought that would be the end of it; she did not think Bobby would stick at it long enough to complete his Valentine for the Queen. But he did—with a little help from Dad—and it had three verses:

Hello to you, my darling Queen,
I love you, whom I've never seen.
Will you be my Valentine?
I'll be yours if you'll be mine.

I'd like to take you out to tea
But that's not possible, I see.
I know that you have got to rule
And me, I've got to go to school.

And so, dear Queen, I'll be content
Just with this Valentine I've sent
And this is what I have to say—
A happy, happy Valentine's Day.

In the end, Bobby did not post his Valentine to the Queen. He did not have the money for the stamp! It is a pity, for I think the Queen might have been rather pleased to receive Bobby's Valentine.

Bobby received one or two Valentine cards himself — and he was very pleased. And no wonder, because it is exciting to know that someone loves you, even if you do not know who that someone is.

Valentines are meant to be what we call 'anonymous', that is to say we don't know who has sent them. That is a secret. But the most important love message of all is no secret. God sent Jesus into the world to let us know that He loves us. He wants us all to know it.

That is the best Valentine message in the world!

BOBBY WINS THE RACE

Bobby beat me in a race one day when I called at his house. He knew I was coming and I realised afterwards that he had been thinking about it and making his plans and preparations for it.

Bobby, you see, likes games and competitions. When he gets the chance, he likes to play them against me — and he likes nothing better than to win!

On this particular day Bobby was determined to beat me and he had his plans well laid. After we had been chatting for a time out in the garden — for it was a nice, sunny day — Bobby suddenly said to me: "I could beat you in a race."

"I think, Bobby," I replied, "that I'm too big and strong for a little boy like you to beat me."

But Bobby was determined. "If you will just give me a start, I think I can beat you."

"I am afraid, Bobby," I laughed, "you would need an awfully big start before you could beat me."

"No, no," replied Bobby. "If you just give me one step of a start and let me choose *where* the race is to be, I will beat you."

"Right you are, Bobby," I said, "I'll take you on. I'm quite sure I can beat you wherever the race takes place. I'll even give you five or six steps of a start."

"One step is all I need," replied Bobby. He spoke with such smug confidence that for the very first time I began to wonder what I had let myself in for.

"Let's get on with it," I said. "I'll have to be on my way soon. Where's this great race going to be run—round the garden?"

"Not round the garden," Bobby answered, "but *in* the garden. Just wait here a minute." And off he ran. I was still trying to puzzle this out when back he came, dragging a ladder behind him. As I watched him, wondering what was in his mind, Bobby propped the ladder against the garage wall. "There you are," he said with great glee, "that's where our race is to be run—up that ladder—and you promised me a step of a start."

As soon as he had said this, he took up position with both feet firmly on the first step of the ladder.

"I'm all ready to start," he cried. "Do you admit that I must beat you?"

Of course I had to declare him the winner. There was no way I could pass him, so long as he kept his feet on the ladder.

I could not help admiring the little rascal's cleverness, and I could not help thinking at the same time that, if we put our feet on the ladder of Christian faith and keep them there, nothing can defeat us.

BOBBY AND THE THUNDERSTORM

Bobby can sometimes misbehave quite badly. Sometimes, his mother says, it is just as if something got into his head and twisted everything round the wrong way. When he is like that, nothing pleases him at all, and he can be a real trial to Mum and Dad with his grumbles and complaints.

There was a day like that not so long ago. For most of it, Bobby had been in a bad temper and it grew even worse when they sat down to their evening meal. When the sweet was served — a rather lovely trifle — Bobby seemed determined to make a scene.

"Take it away," he shouted, "I don't want trifle tonight. I want ice-cream."

"There is no ice-cream tonight," said his mother quietly. "Eat your trifle like a good boy."

"No, I won't," said Bobby, "I want ice-cream. I want

ice-cream."

Bobby's Dad decided he was not going to put up with Bobby's tantrums any longer.

"Bobby," he said in a very stern voice, "I will give you one more chance. Are you going to eat your trifle or not?"

"I'm not," said Bobby defiantly.

"Right," said Dad, "it will be put in the fridge and you will get nothing else to eat until you eat that trifle. Now get off to bed and be sure when you say your prayers that you ask God to forgive you. He must be displeased with you, the way you have behaved tonight in refusing to eat your trifle."

So the trifle went into the fridge, and Bobby went to bed.

Not long after he fell asleep a fierce thunderstorm broke out. The thunder made such a loud noise that it woke Bobby up. He lay awake for a time while the peals of thunder grew louder and louder, and the lightning flashes got brighter and brighter. They seemed to get nearer and nearer until it was as if they were right inside Bobby's bedroom.

Bobby felt himself getting more and more frightened. Suddenly he got out of bed and began to make his way downstairs and into the kitchen. His dad heard him and went into the kitchen after him. As Dad entered the kitchen, he saw Bobby open the fridge and take out his trifle, and he heard him muttering to himself, "*What* a fuss to make about a plate of trifle."

Bobby thought that God had sent the thunderstorm as a punishment for his bad behaviour. But that is not how God works. God does not punish us like that for our wrong-doing or, as the Bible calls it, our sin. It hurts God when we do wrong and He is sorry about it. But He still loves us. All He wants is that we should be sorry too.

When we are sorry for our sins and ask God to forgive them, He does so at once.

BOBBY HAS TUMMY-ACHE

When Bobby came in for his lunch one day last week, he was in a frightful hurry. He had been playing all morning with his chum Jimmy, and they had been having great fun. They were just on the point of setting out on yet another daring voyage into outer space when Bobby's mum put her head out of the front door. She called out, "Bobby, your lunch is ready. Come and get it," and she disappeared inside again.

Bobby did not see why he should let a little thing like lunch keep him back from the important space flight he was due to make and so he and Jimmy set off on their journey. A minute or two later, his mum put her head out of the front door again. This time she said, "Bobby, did you not hear me say that your lunch is ready? Come in *this minute.*" Bobby knew that when his mum spoke in *that* voice, she really meant what she said and, although he was already halfway to the moon, he said to Jimmy: "I'll be back in a minute" and ran into the house.

Bobby was so excited and so anxious to go back out to play that he could hardly eat anything. Very soon he said: "Mum, I can't eat anything more. Please may I leave the table and go back out to play?" With a sigh, his mum said, "All right, but you are a very foolish boy not to take your lunch properly. I am afraid that you will be very hungry before long."

Bobby was not worried about that and dashed out to complete his trip to the moon. He was happy then, but he was not so happy later in the afternoon. He came into the house with his hands clasped over his tummy and looking very sorry for himself. "Mum," he wailed, "I have an awful pain in my tummy."

"I am not surprised," said Mum. "This is what you get for not eating your lunch. Your tummy is empty and that is what is making it ache. I am just going to make a meal. Once you get something in it, you will find that your tummy is better again."

Sure enough it turned out just as Mum had said it would. As soon as Bobby had something to eat, the pain in his tummy disappeared.

That same evening, before Bobby had gone off to bed, the minister called. Bobby opened the door to him and invited him in. As they walked through to the living-room, the minister said to Bobby, "How are you keeping, Bobby?"

"I am fine," replied Bobby. "How are you?"

"I am fine, too," said the minister, "except that I have rather a sore head at the moment."

"Oh, don't worry about that," Bobby answered. "That's just because your head is empty. Once you get something in it, the pain will go away."

Bobby's mum was terribly embarrassed to hear Bobby say this, but the minister thought it was a great joke and laughed heartily.

An empty head would be a dreadful thing to have. But there is something much worse, and that is an empty heart. If you will let him, however, Jesus will come in and fill your heart with love and goodness and beauty.

BOBBY NEVER GIVES UP

Bobby and Mum were not on very good terms with each other. Bobby had been rather difficult most of the afternoon and Mum felt she had had as much as she could stand. She had taken Bobby with her into town to do some shopping and the trouble had all begun when she had decided to stop for a cup of tea. In the tea room she had ordered tea for herself and a glass of milk for Bobby, but when his milk arrived Bobby turned up his nose.

"I want lemonade," he said.

"There isn't any lemonade," his mum replied, "and in any case I have ordered milk. Be a good boy and drink it up." But Bobby began to sulk and refused to drink his milk.

He continued to sulk for the rest of the afternoon and refused to be pleased with anything his mum said or did. He was at his very worst by the time Mum decided to go home and he caused quite a commotion when they were standing waiting for the bus.

As soon as Dad came home that evening, Mum told him the whole tale of Bobby's misbehaviour. Dad was very angry. "When your meal is finished, Bobby," he said, "you will get washed and go straight upstairs to bed." To be packed off early to bed was the worst punishment Bobby could have, especially in the summer-time. But, although he was still in a bad mood, he knew better than to argue with his dad.

Bobby got washed and made his way upstairs to bed. Dad came with him and, after he had listened to Bobby say his prayers, he said, "Now, get off to sleep as soon as you can and don't let us hear another word out of you tonight."

Not long after Dad had come back downstairs, Bobby was heard shouting, "Can I have a drink of water?"

"No," Dad called, "you are in disgrace. Go to sleep."

A little later, Bobby's voice was heard again, "Please, can I have a drink of water? I am very thirsty."

Dad was really angry this time. "I am not telling you again, Bobby," he said. "You are *not* to have a drink of water and, if I have another word out of you tonight, I will give you a smacking."

There was silence for a little and then Bobby's voice came downstairs once more, "My throat is awfully dry. Can I have a drink of water?"

"Bobby," Dad thundered, "I warned you what would happen. I am coming upstairs to smack you."

There was a slight pause, and then Bobby spoke again. "Well, if you are coming up to smack me, will you bring a drink of water with you?"

Persistence is sometimes wrong. Bobby's was on this occasion. But it can be useful. It depends why you are being persistent. If you are persistent about something which is wrong, it is a *bad* way to behave; but if you are persistent about something which is right, it is a very *good* way to behave. What we all have to be persistent in is trying to live as Jesus wants us to live. That is something never to be given up.

BOBBY'S BIRTHDAY

It was Bobby's birthday yesterday and I can tell you that he has been anticipating it for weeks. He was looking forward to the party he was going to have and to the presents which he hoped to get! In particular, Bobby wondered what his Aunt Mary would send him this year.

Aunt Mary is very fond of Bobby and very kind to him. She always gives him a very good present for his birthday. In fact, Aunt Mary's birthday present to him was always the one that Bobby liked best, so he wondered eagerly what it would turn out to be on this occasion.

As his birthday drew nearer, Bobby started to worry about Aunt Mary and her present. What if Aunt Mary did not remember his birthday? After all, there was a whole year between his last birthday and this one. She could easily forget in that time. Bobby was really concerned, and thought how awful it would be if Aunt Mary's present did not come.

In the end Bobby decided to write a letter to Aunt Mary. It took a long time. He had to wrinkle his brow a great deal, and lick his pencil many times. But at last it was finished in the very best writing he could manage, and this is what it said.

Dear Aunt Mary,

I am very sorry that I forgot about your birthday last month and did not send you a present. It really was very bad of me and I cannot blame you if you forget my birthday which is next Saturday.

    love,
      Bobby

Now what do you think of that?

Aunt Mary's present arrived all right and it was just as fine a present as the others had been. But of course, you know as well as I do that Aunt Mary's present would have come just the same even if Bobby had not sent his letter to remind her.

Jesus never needs to be reminded of us and of our needs. For he loves us too well ever to forget us—even though sometimes we forget him.

Passion Sunday

BOBBY AND A FAMOUS PICTURE

Bobby went with his mum yesterday afternoon when she went to do some shopping. Little boys often hate going shopping with their mums, but Bobby actually likes it. He likes to see the people and the shops and he just loves to get his nose pressed up against a window so that he can gaze at what is inside.

Yesterday was no exception. Everytime he got the chance, 'plop' went his nose up against a shop window and he looked and looked—until his mum dragged him away.

In one of the shop windows, Bobby saw a picture which interested him very much. It was a copy of a very famous painting, called 'The Light of the World'. Perhaps you may have seen a copy of this painting somewhere and know what it is like. (I have seen the original painting and so I know what it is like.) It shows Jesus, with a crown of thorns on his head and carrying a lantern in his hand, standing outside a door. He has just knocked on the door.

Bobby looked at this picture very closely and then he pulled his mum's coat and said, "That's Jesus, isn't it?" "Yes, Bobby," his mum replied, "that is Jesus." "What is he doing?" asked Bobby. "He wants to get into that house," answered Bobby's mum, "but the door has no handle on the outside and so Jesus can get in only when the people inside open the door to him." "Oh, Mum," cried Bobby, and his voice was sad. "Why don't they let him in?"

It seemed terrible to Bobby that anyone should keep Jesus standing outside, even for a moment. It is. Yet that is what some of us do.

Today we are remembering how Jesus died for us on the Cross of Calvary. He allowed himself to be killed like that because he loves us. That was the only way he could bring us new life. Now this Jesus who was crucified for our sakes and who is alive again (because he rose from the dead on Easter Day) is knocking on the door of *your* life. He wants to come in to be your Saviour and your Friend.

Will *you* open the door?

Palm Sunday

BOBBY AND THE DONKEY

Bobby had never seen a donkey until yesterday. He and his dad were out for a walk in the afternoon when Bobby saw this strange and funny animal with long ears and an odd appearance. He was very interested in it and when they came alongside it, he said to his father, "Dad, what is the name of that funny animal?" "That is a donkey," his dad replied.

At once Bobby's face changed. His cheeks became very red and then he began to cry. "What on earth is the matter?" his dad asked in alarm. "Why are you crying?" "Well, Dad," sobbed Bobby, "a boy at school yesterday called me a donkey and now I know what he meant. I did not know that a donkey was an ugly, stupid beast."

"Now, Bobby," said his dad, "there is really no need to be upset and, if you will stop crying, I will tell you why." So Bobby sniffed hard, took out his handkerchief and wiped his face, sniffed hard again, looked up at this father and waited for him to speak.

"It is true," his dad began, "that the donkey is a rather peculiar looking animal, but it is also a very famous animal, for a donkey was a great help to Jesus one day when he was on earth. It was the first Palm Sunday, and Jesus wanted to enter the city of Jerusalem in a way that would show the world that he was the King of love and of peace. The best way he could think of doing this was for him to ride into the city on a donkey's back and that is just what he did. On the first Palm Sunday, with hundreds and hundreds of people lining the road, shouting and cheering, it was on a donkey's back that Jesus came into Jerusalem. So you see, Bobby, the donkey is not something to laugh at but something to admire because of its part in that great story."

Bobby did not mind now that he had been called a donkey.

Because a donkey gave such important help to Jesus on the first Palm Sunday, somebody once wrote a famous poem about it. It is a grown-ups' poem and difficult for children to understand, but here it is. Perhaps when you are older, you will read it for yourselves.

When fishes flew and forests walked
And figs grew upon thorn,
Some moment when the moon was blood
Then surely I was born.
With monstrous head and sickening cry

And ears like errant wings,
The devil's walking parody
On all four-footed things.
The tattered outlaw of the earth,
Of ancient crooked will;
Starve, scourge, deride me: I am dumb,
I keep my secret still.
Fools! For I also had my hour;
One far fierce hour and sweet:
There was a shout about my ears,
And palms before my feet.

G.K. Chesterton

The donkey is a very humble creature, yet it was of great service to Jesus. You and I, too, no matter how small or unimportant we may seem to be, can be of great service to Jesus if we will let him use us.

Easter Sunday

BOBBY LIKES SURPRISES

Bobby likes very much to get a surprise—as long as it is a pleasant surprise. For instance, you can see him smiling all over his face if his football team wins when he has not expected it to happen. If he gets a surprise present from anybody, which sometimes happens, he is absolutely delighted.

It was because Bobby enjoys pleasant surprises that he was so willing to join with Dad's plan to give Mum a big surprise on her birthday. Dad's plan was for himself, Bobby and Susan to pretend to have forgotten all about the birthday. They would get up on her birthday and just act as if it was an ordinary day. They would not wish her a happy birthday. They would not give her any cards or presents. Then, at lunchtime, when Mum would likely be feeling disappointed, they would spring their big surprise.

That is just what they did.

Naturally, when nothing at all was said about her birthday in the morning, Mum really thought they had all forgotten it. She was disappointed and sad, but did not say anything. When lunchtime came and she was in the kitchen attending to the meal, she heard Dad call out. "Mum," he said, "come through to the dining-room and see this strange thing Susan and Bobby have got hold of."

Mum rushed through, wondering what was wrong. There were Susan and Bobby holding a birthday cake with icing and candles. Dad, Bobby and Susan began to sing 'Happy Birthday' and when they had finished singing, they handed Mum a beautiful new handbag for her birthday present (they knew she had wanted one for a long time).

What a lovely surprise that was for Mum! She had thought her birthday was going to be an unhappy one because it has been forgotten, but now it had turned out to be one of the happiest she had ever had, for when something has a surprise good ending, after it looked like being a disappointment, that makes it all the happier.

Easter reminds us of the most wonderful 'surprise ending' in all the world. When Jesus was crucified to death on the first Good Friday, that looked like the end of his story, a very sad end. All his friends were broken-hearted. Then God raised Jesus from the dead and made him alive again. What had seemed to be a terrible disaster was turned into a glorious victory.

That is why Easter is the 'gladdest' day in the whole year.

Low Sunday

BOBBY LOVES EASTER

Bobby was so pleased with the party Mum and Dad had for him on the day he was five. It was marvellous and he enjoyed it very much. But the day after his birthday, he said a rather strange thing.

"Mum," he said, "now that my birthday is over, does that mean I am only four again?"

"No, no," laughed Mum, "once you have a birthday, you never go back to the age you were before. The day of your fifth birthday is over and the party is over, but being five is never over until you become six."

Bobby was so glad, because he did not want to be four again. And he was very glad when he discovered it was the same with Easter Day.

Bobby liked it very much in church on Easter Sunday. The church was filled with lovely yellow daffodils. The choir sang joyful, happy music. The hymns were very bright and the minister told them that this was the most wonderful day in the whole year, because it was on this day that Jesus had been raised to life again from the dead.

It was the first time Bobby had sat through the church service on an Easter Day and he thought it was wonderful. The following day he said to his mum, "Mum, it is a pity that Easter is only one day in the year. It's such a happy day with such a happy message."

"Yes," said Mum, "I know how you feel, but you don't need to be too disappointed because, although there is only one Easter *Day* in the year, the message of Easter is true *every* day of the year."

It is. What good news that is! There is only one Easter Day each year, but the message of Easter—the message that Jesus is alive—is true for *every* day of every year!

BOBBY AND MR NOBODY

Does Mr Nobody ever come to stay in your house? He sometimes comes to stay in Bobby's house, and he was there all last week. Mr Nobody is not a real person, of course. He is the make-believe person that boys and girls often blame for the wrong things they themselves have done. Yes, Mr Nobody was certainly at Bobby's house all last week.

On Monday, Mum discovered the pantry door lying open and the lid off the biscuit tin, and she was sure that some of her special chocolate biscuits had disappeared. "Bobby," she said, "who has been taking the biscuits?" "Nobody has been taking the biscuits," said Bobby—and that was the first thing for which Mr Nobody was blamed.

On Tuesday, when Dad came home from work, he found that someone had plucked nearly all of his favourite flowers out of the front garden and left them lying on the path. He was furious and, rushing into the house, he said, "Bobby, who has been meddling with my good flowers?" "Nobody has been meddling with your good flowers," replied Bobby—and that was the second thing for which Mr Nobody was blamed.

On Wednesday, when Mum went into the lounge to tidy it up, there was one of her favourite ornaments lying broken in the hearth, just as if someone had accidentally knocked it over. "Bobby," she called, "who knocked over my ornament and broke it?" Bobby called back, "Nobody knocked over your ornament and broke it"—and that was the third thing for which Mr Nobody was blamed.

On Thursday, only ten minutes after she had finished washing the kitchen floor, Mum discovered a trail of muddy footprints right across it. "Bobby," she asked, "who was walking on my clean floor with muddy feet?" "Nobody," said Bobby, "was walking on your clean floor with muddy feet"—and that was the fourth thing for which Mr Nobody was blamed that week.

On Friday, Mum discovered the bath filled with water and water spilled all over the bathroom floor, just as if someone had been sailing his toy boats in the bath. "Bobby," she said, "who has been making all this mess on the bathroom floor?" Bobby answered, "Nobody has been making all this mess on the bathroom floor"—and that was the fifth thing for which Mr Nobody was blamed.

On Friday night Mum and Dad had a private talk about all these happenings. They knew of course that it was really Bobby who had been doing them all but they wanted Bobby to own up, for he was only making his misbehaviour worse by denying it. At last Dad said, "I have a plan and I think it will work."

The family had arranged an outing to the Zoo for that Saturday, but when breakfast was over Dad said, "I don't think we will be able to go to the Zoo today after all." "Oh!", said Bobby, in great disappointment, "Why can't we go?" "It's this fellow, Mr Nobody," said Dad. "Look what he has been up to this week. If we left him alone all day, there might be no house left when we returned." "But," said Bobby, "Mr Nobody is not a real person. He did not do any of these things." "Mr Nobody is not a real person?", said Dad, "Well then, who has been doing all the bad things that have been done this week?" "Me," admitted Bobby, "I did them all."

They did go to the Zoo, but I can tell you that Bobby got a good talking-to before they set out — and he deserved every word of it. It was bad enough to do the things he did, but it was twice as bad to refuse to admit them.

Lots of boys and girls (and grown-ups too) are often like Bobby and blame Mr Nobody for things they have done themselves. But Jesus wants us, when we have done wrong, not to deny it or try to blame it on someone else, but to own up to it.

That is what is called 'confessing our sins'. It is only when we do that, that Jesus can help us with our failings. When we admit to him that we have done wrong but are sorry for it, he will forgive us and help us.

BOBBY'S PRESENT TO DAD

Bobby's dad's birthday was last week, so Bobby gave him a present. But there is a story behind the gift!

Some weeks ago, Mum said to Bobby, "Dad's birthday will soon be here and if you wish to give him a present you ought to begin saving up for it now." Bobby nodded his head vigorously to show that he agreed, but then, I am afraid, he forgot all about it. One day last week Mum said to him, "Tomorrow is Dad's birthday. Have you bought his present?"

Bobby had not even remembered about it! Hurriedly he began to empty his pockets to see what money he had. Those pockets contained all sorts of things—pieces of string, a rubber, bus tickets, crayons and a whole lot more —but there was only 5p there. "How can I buy a birthday present with that?" he said. "What am I to do?"

Bobby thought and thought. Then he had an idea. "I know," he said to himself, "I'll take a collection for Dad's present." So off he went to Mum. "Mum," he said, "I am taking a collection for Dad's birthday present. What will you give me?"

"I will give you nothing," said Mum, "I warned you about the birthday. If I gave you the money for it, the present would not really be yours. You will just need to take some money out of your piggy-bank."

"Oh, no," replied Bobby, "I can't do that. That money is for my holidays." Away he went to see his little sister, Susan.

"Do you have any money?" he asked her.

"Yes, please," she replied.

"What do you mean, 'Yes, please'?" he enquired. "I asked you if you had any money."

"Oh," answered Susan, "I thought you said, 'Do you want any money?'"

Bobby still had no money collected for Dad's present, and the only other person he could ask was Dad himself. This was a bit awkward but there was nothing else for it, so Bobby marched along to Dad and said, "Dad, I am taking a collection for a good cause. Will you give me something for it?"

"What good cause is it?" Dad wanted to know.

"I can't tell you that," said Bobby, "but it really is a good cause."

But Dad was not very sure about it. "If you will not tell me what the collection is for, I am afraid I can give you no more than 10p."

So Bobby now had fifteen pence with which to buy Dad's birthday present. He thought about it for a time and then went and made his purchase. The following morning he said to Dad, "Many happy returns", and handed him a parcel. When Dad unwrapped the parcel, he found that Bobby had given him a packet of potato crisps.

"Thanks very much," said Dad, although really he was rather surprised.

"I would have liked," Bobby said, "to buy something more expensive, but I did not have enough money. It's really your fault. If you had put more into the collection I was making, you would have got more back."

That was true—although it was hardly fair to blame Dad!

The same is true of many things in life. The more we put into them, the more they will give us back. This is true also of the service of Jesus. The more we put into that of our love and our enthusiasm and our loyalty, the more it will give back to us in excitement and happiness.

Mothering Sunday

BOBBY AND HIS MUM

Lots of people get fun out of looking through old snapshots. Do you?

One rainy Saturday when it was too wet for Bobby to be allowed outside to play, his mum gave him a whole drawerful of photographs to look at to pass the time. Bobby loved it. There were all sorts of photographs. Some had been taken at home or near home. Some had been taken on holidays. Some had been taken quite a long time ago. Some had been taken recently.

Some were of people Bobby did not know. Many were of people Bobby did know, but there were some of these that he did not recognise at once. There was one, for instance, of a baby. Bobby looked at it and scratched his head.

"I wonder who that is," he said to himself. "I am sure

I have not seen that baby before. I wonder who it can be?" "Mum," he called, "who is this baby?" Mum came over to look, and laughed. "Why, Bobby," she said, "that is *you* when you were only six months old."

Bobby had to laugh at not knowing himself! Then he went on looking at one photograph after another. When he came to one which was bigger than the rest, Bobby could tell that it was a very special one. It was a photograph of a wedding with everyone looking very smart and everyone smiling happily and the bride there in her lovely white wedding-dress. "That's a really lovely picture," Bobby thought to himself as he looked at it more closely.

"Oh," he said, "I know these people. There's my dad and that's my mum in the white dress." "Mum," he called, "come and see *this* photograph. You and Dad are in it."

Mum looked at the photograph. "Yes," she said, "that was taken when your dad and I got married."

"I see," said Bobby. "So that was the day when you came here to work for Dad and me."

That is not what wedding days are really meant to be. It is hardly a case of the bride signing on to work for her husband and children! But that is what a mother does all the same. She works and works for her family so that their lives will be as good and as happy as she can make them.

That is why we have a special Mothering Sunday each year. It is a day for saying thanks to God for all the love *your* mother has shown *you*.

At the same time we should thank God for *His* love because it never fails.

BOBBY FINDS JESUS AT THE SEASIDE

Bobby was going to his aunt for the weekend. She lived at the seaside and Bobby was delighted. He thought it was great fun and he was looking forward very much to playing on the beach when he got there. As a matter of fact, he rather thought that he had nothing else to do but to arrive and go straight out on to the beach to play.

But that was not how it turned out, and Bobby was not a bit pleased. When they arrived at his aunt's house, Mum said: "Now, Bobby, it's been a long day for you. As soon as you've had something to eat, you must get washed and off to bed as quickly as possible. It's past your usual bedtime. If you don't get to sleep soon, you'll be far too tired tomorrow to enjoy yourself."

Mum was right, of course. It *was* past Bobby's usual bed-time, and he did need his sleep. But Bobby did not feel tired and he wanted to get to the beach as soon as ever he could.

"Can't I go and play on the beach first?" he asked.

"No," said Mum, "it's much too late. You can be on the beach first thing in the morning, but not tonight."

"Can I not go and play on the beach just for five minutes?" pleaded Bobby.

"No," replied Mum, a little louder, and a little more

firmly this time, because she knew only too well what Bobby's 'five minutes' could be like. "You are going to bed."

Bobby was very, very cross because he could not get his own way and he went into the sulks. It was a lovely meal that his aunt had ready for them, but Bobby grumbled and complained all the way through it and hardly ate anything.

Mum got more and more angry with Bobby, but she tried to be patient with him because they were on holiday. She kept hoping that he would get over it soon and be his usual cheery self again. But things got worse and worse, and at last Mum's patience came to an end.

When he was having his bath, Bobby deliberately splashed a whole lot of water right out of the bath and on to the bathroom floor.

"Bobby," said Mum, "I've had enough of your bad behaviour. You've been a dreadful boy since we arrived here. Jesus must be very disappointed to see you behaving like this."

Bobby looked around the bathroom in surprise. "Jesus?" he asked, "has Jesus come to the seaside too?"

Jesus, of course, does not need to *come* to the seaside. He is there already. We cannot see him, but Jesus is there wherever we go, offering his friendship and help.

BOBBY LOSES THE POWER OF HIS LEGS

Bobby can dress himself. He has been able to do it for quite a long time. He always dresses himself when he is going to school. Mum wakes him up, then leaves him to it and Bobby puts his clothes on all by himself. Bobby doesn't need any help.

That is why Mum got such a shock one morning when, after she had wakened Bobby and come downstairs, there was a terrible scream from Bobby's bedroom.

"Mum, help," he was yelling at the top of his voice, "help me, help me." Then he began to cry.

Mum was already running up the stairs. "What's wrong?" she called. "What has happened?"

"I can't walk," Bobby called out between sobs. "My legs have lost their power. They're useless."

When Mum burst into the bedroom, she was in tears herself wondering what awful illness might have come upon her son. She felt even worse when she saw Bobby lying on the floor not able to get up, the tears streaming down his face. Then she realised what was wrong, and she started to laugh. She was so relieved she just could not stop laughing. This made poor Bobby more upset than ever.

"That's terrible, Mum," he wailed, "laughing at me when my legs are paralysed!"

"No, Bobby," said Mum, "your legs are not paralysed. Here, I'll soon put you right." She lifted him up on to his bed, took off his trousers and put them back on again.

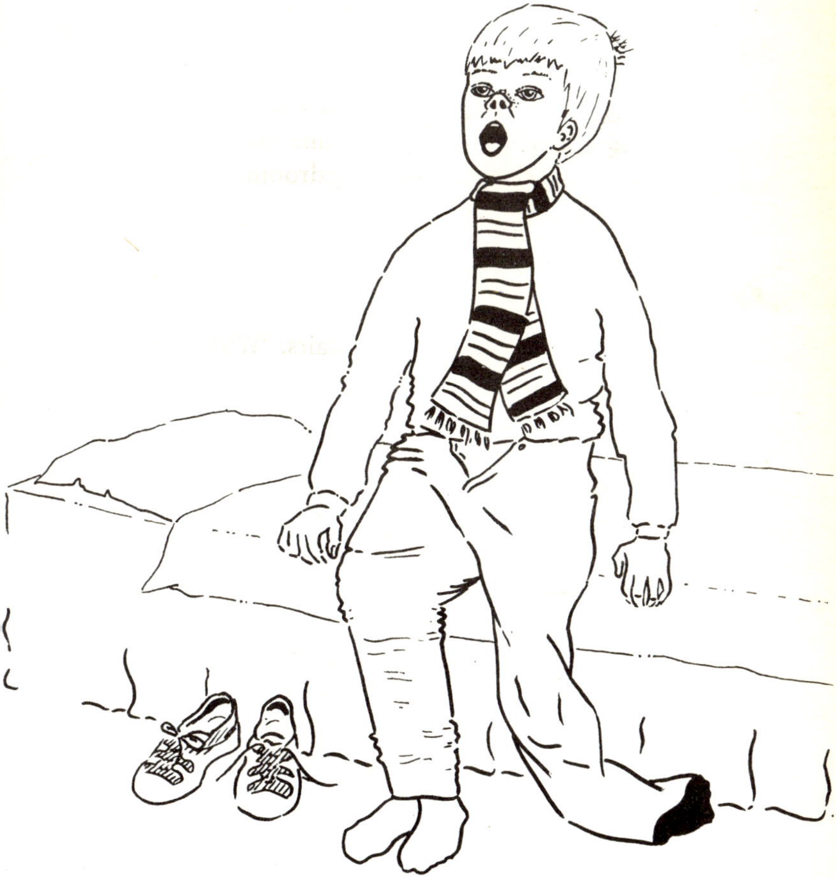

And Bobby found that he could stand up and walk about without any trouble. His legs were all right again.

When Bobby sat on the side of his bed as usual to put on his trousers, he had made a mistake and put both feet into the same trouser leg. Then when he tried to stand up and walk, he just fell down on the floor.

The trouble was that Bobby had not taken enough care when he was putting on his trousers, and his careless mistake gave him and his mother a fright they need not have had.

Carelessness can do a lot of damage, both to ourselves and to others. Jesus wants us to take care too, to ensure that we help, not hurt, other people.

BOBBY JUMPS OVER THE HOUSE

Like nearly every little boy, Bobby sometimes goes in for a bit of boasting. Some of his boasting is quite ridiculous. When you hear him at it in this kind of way, you know at once that you must not take him too seriously. That is why his dad just laughed when Bobby came to him one day and said, "Dad, I can jump ever so high. I could jump over our house."

"You could jump over our house?" said Dad, "I think I would need to see that before I believed it."

"Well, then," said Bobby triumphantly, "I will let you see me doing it."

This is going to be worth watching, Dad thought to himself. He watched as Bobby got a sheet of writing paper and a pencil. On the paper he wrote 'Our House'. Then he laid the paper on the floor—and jumped over it.

"There you are, Dad," he called out in high glee, "I've jumped over Our House, haven't I?" And Dad had to admit that he had, although it was not quite what he had been expecting.

Dad had thought Bobby was making a very boastful promise which he could not possibly keep. But it was a trick.

Jesus makes a lot of marvellous promises about lots of things. Some people have thought these promises were just empty promises, which he could not possibly keep. But the promises of Jesus are not like that. Jesus carries out the promises he makes. We can trust all of them.

BOBBY HAS A 'SHARES' PROBLEM

I am sorry to have to tell you that Bobby is sometimes a very selfish boy, especially where his little sister is concerned. He thinks that he should have the better part of everything and that she should always have the worse part. He thinks that he should always be first to sit down at table, first to have his bath, first to be dressed if they are going out, first to climb into Dad's car, first to see the comic papers, first to reach the postman—first to have everything. Bobby thinks, too, that he should be allowed to play with Susan's toys whenever he feels like it, but that she should never be allowed to touch his.

He thinks also that he should always have a bigger share than his little sister of anything good that might be going. One day last week, for instance, Bobby knew that there was some fudge in the house. "Mum," he asked, "may I have a piece of fudge, please?" And because he had asked so nicely, Mum said at once, "Yes, Bobby, you may. You will find a piece on the pantry shelf. Fetch it and divide it between Susan and yourself."

Bobby wasted no time in fetching the piece of fudge, and then he broke it in two. But what a job he made of breaking it! One of the pieces was very large and one was very small. However, this did not seem to worry Bobby very much. Without the slightest hesitation he handed the small piece to his little sister and kept the large piece to himself.

Mum had noticed what was going on, and she began to scold Bobby. "That was a selfish thing to do, keeping the larger piece for yourself," she said. "That is not how Jesus would like you to behave. In fact, when you have first choice, you ought always to take the smaller piece of whatever it is."

A little later Mum thought she would test Bobby to see if he had learned this lesson properly. "Bobby," she called, "here are two apples. There is one for you and one for Susan. Share them out."

Bobby took the apples from Mum and discovered that one was large and one was small. For a moment he stood looking at them with a puzzled frown, but then his face cleared and, holding the apples out to his little sister, Bobby said, "Take an apple and remember that the person who has first choice must take the smaller one."

That was quite clever of Bobby, but it was also very selfish; and selfish is something that Jesus does not want us to be. Selfishness is thinking of ourselves before other people. Jesus himself was, of course, never selfish. He always thought of others first. We must all do that.

BOBBY RUNS AWAY FROM HOME

Bobby and his mum fell out last week. That is not, perhaps, the right way to put it, for the 'falling-out' was all on Bobby's side.

Bobby has days, as you know, when he is inclined to be peevish and this was one of them. Things had not gone too well at school that afternoon. At any rate when Bobby arrived home from school, he was in a very bad temper.

He stamped into the house, flung his school-bag into a corner and shouted, "When will dinner be ready? I'm hungry."

"You know perfectly well," said Mum, "that dinner will not be ready for more than an hour yet. There is no need to make such a fuss."

"But I'm hungry *now*," said Bobby, quite crossly. "I want my dinner now."

"Don't be so silly and so bad-tempered," replied Mum. "You may have a biscuit now if you ask for it properly, but dinner will be at the usual time."

Bobby, I am afraid, was now in a real temper. "You don't love me," he shouted, "Nobody cares if I starve to death. I think I will just . . ." He stopped for a moment as he considered what terribly wicked thing he could do to show how angry he was, and then he burst out, "I think I will just run away this minute."

He had no sooner said this than he rushed out and banged the door behind him. Once through the front gate he dashed along the street as fast as his legs would carry him. He kept on running until he came to the end of the street. When he got there, he stopped for a minute then turned right round and ran back to his own gate. Then he turned round again and ran all the way back to the end of the street. Once more he turned and ran back along the street to his own gate.

This went on for quite some time — Bobby running along the street and back again. It went on, indeed, until on Bobby's ninth journey, the man next door stopped him and said, "Here, Bobby, I've been watching you running to the end of the street and back, over and over again. What are you doing?"

"I'm running away from home," said Bobby.

"You're running away from home?" said the man-next-door. "It seems to be a funny way to run away from home. If I were running away from home, I wouldn't turn back when I reached the end of the street, I'd keep right on."

"That's all very well for you," answered Bobby, "but I'm not allowed to cross the road by myself."

Bobby was so angry and cross that he thought he would do something very wicked out of spite. But when it came to the point, he remembered what he had been taught in his home and that saved him from doing something he had been taught not to do.

Often when boys and girls grow up to be men and women, there come times when something makes them angry or resentful or disappointed. When that happens, they may feel like doing something wicked 'out of spite', but they may also be saved from that wickedness by remembering something they have learned about Jesus in the house of God.

As you come week by week to God's house—to church service and to Sunday School—you are always being taught something about Jesus and his love and the way he wants you to live. The more you learn about him and the more you remember it, the less likely you are to let your life be spoiled and disfigured by wicked things.

BOBBY 'STUMPS' HIS FRIENDS

Bobby and his friends were playing 'Guesses'. They were gathered around a sweet-shop window and were taking it in turns to 'give a guess'. The one who was giving the guess picked out some object from those in the window and called out the first letter of its name. The others had then to guess what the object was and the first one to guess correctly gave the next object.

It came to be Bobby's turn to give a guess. He looked and looked into the window and he thought and thought. Then, making up his mind all at once, he called out "T". Immediately the others began searching the window busily with their eyes to try and find out what this could be. "Toffee?" said one. "No," said Bobby. "Treacle," said another. "No," said Bobby.

Several more guesses were made but everyone was wrong. Then there came two or three minutes' silence as the 'guessers' tried to catch sight of something else that began with "T". But in the end they had to give up. "You'll have to tell us, Bobby," they said, "we can't get it. What does 'T' stand for?"

Triumphantly, Bobby shouted, "Taramels!"

Well, Bobby stumped his friends all right, but they did not have much chance, did they? He had given them the wrong first letter and that, of course, put them right off the track.

I do not suppose we can blame Bobby too much. After all he is only five, and since he calls caramels 'taramels', he thought that 'T' really was the first letter. So we can't blame Bobby *too* much, but his mistake still spoilt the guessing game for his friends. As the beginning was wrong, they had not much chance of getting the object right!

Beginnings are always important. If you want to make a good job of anything, it always helps to start well. Of nothing is this more true than it is of our lives. Boys and girls are still at the beginning of their lives. If they want to make the best possible job of them, they should give them into the keeping of Jesus *now*.

BOBBY BLAMES GOD

Bobby had one day last week which was just as bad a day as anyone could imagine. From the very beginning nothing went right. To start with, he did not get out of bed as quickly as he should and, when he did rise, he was a good bit later than he ought to have been. This meant that he had to hurry or be late for school yet again. Bobby did not like having to hurry so early in the morning. It made him quite cross and bad-tempered.

Bobby likes to pour his milk for his cornflakes himself but Mum thought she would save him some time by pouring it for him. When Bobby saw what she had done he was furious. "You know," he shouted, "that I like to pour out my own milk! I'm just not going to take any breakfast for that!" And he picked up his school bag and stamped away to school, banging the door behind him.

Things did not go much better for Bobby at school for, in the middle of the morning, teacher told him off for talking to his neighbour. "If I catch you talking again in class, I will need to punish you," she said. But Bobby was in such a cross-patch mood that he said to himself, "I'll talk if I like. I don't care what old teacher says." Inevitably soon afterwards 'old teacher' caught Bobby talking to his neighbour again. "Bobby," she said, "you are a disobedient boy and I must punish you." So Bobby had to write out five times, 'I am sorry I was disobedient'. And that, I am afraid, put him in a worse mood than ever.

When he went home at lunch-time, he was as grumpy as he could be. Nothing pleased him. He grumbled about everything that was put before him and said he did not care for any of it. Mum was glad when his lunch hour was over and he had to go back to school. "I hope," she thought to herself, "that he is behaving much better by the time he comes home again."

But poor Mum was disappointed. When Bobby came back, he was still in a very bad mood and he continued to misbehave. He turned up his nose at what Mum set before him for the evening meal and, when he thought Mum was not looking, he pinched his little sister until she screamed. Mum was well aware of what was going on, however, and she decided that she was not going to put up with any more of Bobby's tantrums.

"Bobby," she said, "I have had enough of your bad temper for one day. You are going to bed this very minute." Mum was as good as her word. Bobby was sent to bed in disgrace.

When she had seen Bobby safely into his bed, Mum stayed with him while he said his prayers. When he had finished, Mum said to Bobby, "Do you remember that part in your prayer when you said 'Lord, please make me a good boy'?" Bobby nodded his head. "Well," said Mum, "you have been making that same prayer every night for a long time and yet look how bad a boy you've been today. What have you to say about that?"

Bobby looked very serious for a few moments and screwed up his eyes (as he always does when he is thinking hard). Then he said, "I am afraid God has been a bit of a failure with me."

Bobby was blaming God for his own naughtiness. He was making out it was God's fault that he was a bad boy. But it was, of course, his fault, not God's. God wants to make us better people, but he cannot do it unless we really want it to happen. If, however, we ask God to make us good and mean it, He will certainly help us to become better.

BOBBY YIELDS TO TEMPTATION

Bobby was at the seaside for his summer holidays and there were some very warm, sunny days. During these days Bobby liked nothing better than to go swimming and he spent most of his time splashing in and out of the sea. But Bobby's mum was always there when he went into the water. Mum was both wise and careful, and she would not let him in swimming by himself. After all, Bobby is only five.

One very hot afternoon — it was the hottest day of all — Mum had to go up to town for a while and leave Bobby on his own. Before she left, she said to Bobby, "While I am away, you must play either at the house here or at the beach" — the beach was about five minutes' walk from where they lived — "but you must not go into the water until I come back. Now remember that, you must not go bathing before I return."

"All right, Mum," said Bobby, and away she went.

When she arrived home again some time later, the first things she saw were Bobby's wet swimming trunks and a towel spread over the back of the garden seat. She was angry.

"Bobby," she called out, "come here at once." When Bobby appeared, she began to give him a severe scolding.

"You are a very naughty boy," she said, "to go in

swimming on your own after I had told you not to do it, and after you had promised. Why did you do it?"

"Well, Mum," said Bobby thoughtfully, "it was like this. I went down to the beach to play on the sand, as you said I could. The sun was so hot and the sea looked so blue and so cool that I was tempted to go in and I could not resist the temptation."

"That is all very well," said Mum, "but how did you happen to have your trunks and your towel with you at the beach in the first place?"

"Oh," replied Bobby, "I thought, before I left the house, that I *might* be tempted and so I took my trunks with me just in case."

Do you see what Bobby was doing? He was *encouraging* temptation. He was making it all the harder for himself to do what was right and all the easier to do what was wrong, and that is a very foolish thing to do.

Everyone of us is tempted to do wrong at times. We need not feel ashamed of that. But we should not encourage our temptations. Jesus wants us not to encourage our temptations, but to ask his help not to yield to them.

BOBBY GETS HIS WELLINGTONS WET

When Bobby was on holiday at the seaside he had some days of very bad weather. On the worst day of all, the rain was coming down in sheets and the wind was blowing hard. As a result, Bobby was not in a very good mood. The rain and the wind had continued all morning and he had never once been able even to put his foot outside the door.

When he had had his lunch the weather was not one bit better, but Bobby was by this time desperate to get outside, even if it was only for a little while. "Mum," he said, "may I go out — I'll put on my rain clothes and my Wellington boots?" This was the twentieth time he had asked his Mum the same thing (he had already asked her nineteen times before his lunch) and Mum was getting a bit tired of saying 'No'. At any rate, this time she said, "All right, but you must be careful."

So Bobby put on his waterproof coat and his waterproof hat and his Wellington boots and out he went into the wind and the rain. As he went out, Mum said, "Now, Bobby, take care not to splash water inside your Wellingtons, for once they are wet inside, they are very difficult to dry." Bobby nodded his head, and off he went.

He thought he would like to go to the boating pond so he made his way there. Well, not directly there, for he wandered about from side to side, splashing his feet in the puddles along the way. In the end he arrived at the boating pond — and the insides of his Wellingtons were still dry!

"I think I will paddle with my Wellingtons at the edge of the pond," said Bobby to himself. "As long as I don't go near the deeper water in the middle, my Wellingtons won't get wet inside." So he stepped down into the pond and began to splash up and down quite happily. After a time he grew a little tired of just staying at the edge of the pond and he started to move a bit nearer the centre. A man happened to be passing just then and when he noticed that the water was more than half-way up Bobby's Welling-

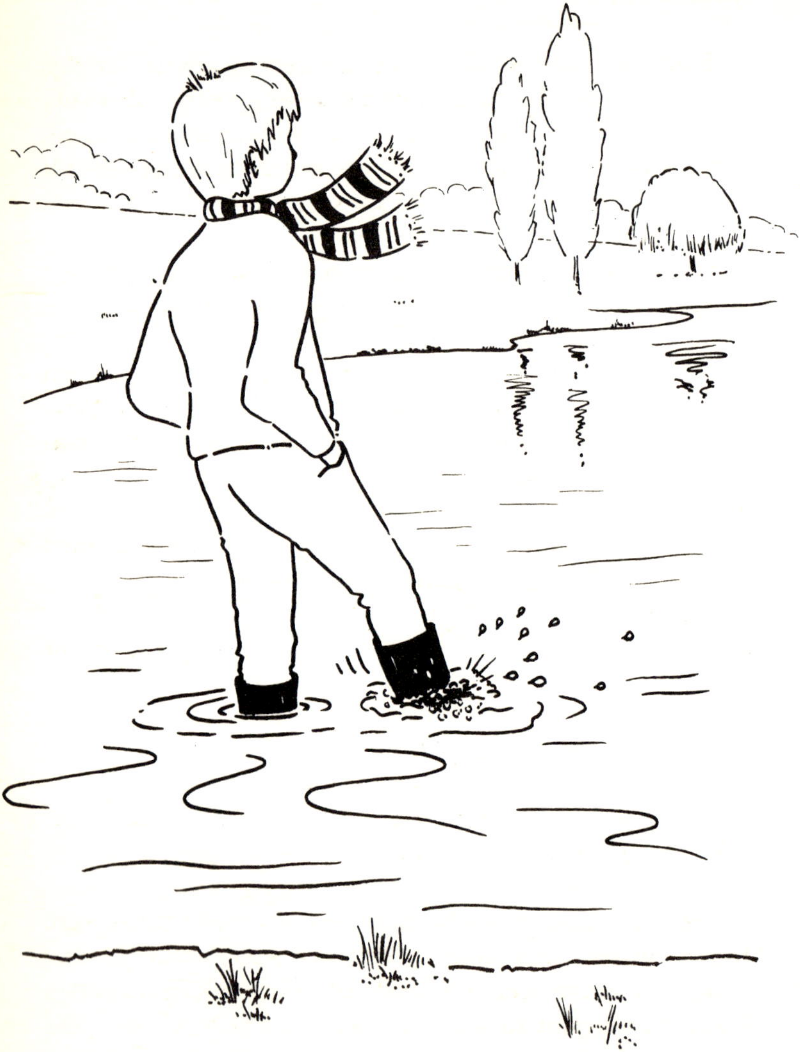

tons, he called to him, "You had better not go any further, Sonny, or you will have the water going over the tops of your boots."

Bobby was not at all pleased at receiving advice like this from a stranger. He thrust out his lower lip and stubbornly continued to splash towards the middle of the pond. "Don't go any further!" said the passer-by in alarm, "it will be too deep."

But Bobby kept on moving as if he had not heard. Just then a fierce gust of wind sent a big wave rolling across the pond. It hit Bobby's Wellingtons with a mighty splash, rolled over their tops and filled them up with water. When the passer-by saw this he said to Bobby, quite angrily, "You are a wicked little boy! You had better get home as fast as you can now."

When Bobby heard this he burst out crying, splashed and sploshed his way to the side of the pond, and began to run home, weeping bitterly all the way. Long before he reached the door, Mum heard him crying and rushed out to see what was the matter.

"What is wrong, Bobby?" she asked.

"I was wading in the pond," Bobby wailed, "and a man called me a wicked little boy."

Just then Mum noticed that Bobby's Wellingtons were full of water. "No wonder he called you 'wicked'," she said, "You have wet the inside of your Wellingtons after I warned you not to do. You really *have* been wicked, and you needn't cry because he called you that."

"But I am not crying because the man called me 'wicked',"

Bobby sobbed, "I am crying because he called me a 'little' boy, for I am a big boy now."

Bobby was not a bit concerned about his wickedness. He was concerned only about being called a little boy. That may seem very silly, yet many of us are just as silly about our wickedness (which, as we know, the Bible calls 'sin'). We are not really worried about being bad. But sin *is* a serious matter, so serious that Jesus came to deal with it — and gave his life for us.

If we tell Jesus that we are sorry for being bad — and really mean it — then he will forgive us and help us to begin again.

BOBBY TAKES THE PLUNGE

It was one of the in-between days of Bobby's holiday, neither a very good one nor a very bad one. Some days were sunny and warm, others were wet and cold. But this was neither sunny nor wet, and neither warm nor cold. It was just an in-between day.

Bobby liked to have a swim in the sea every day, no matter what the weather was like, and he wanted to swim today. He was not allowed to go into the water by himself, so he tried to persuade his dad to go in too. But Dad was not quite as keen as Bobby was. Dad liked to go in swimming when the sun was shining, but he did not care for swimming very much when the sun was out of sight.

"No, Bobby," he said, "I won't bother to go in swimming today. I am afraid the water will be too cold."

"Please, Dad," pleaded Bobby.

"No, Bobby," replied Dad firmly.

Bobby was disappointed and just a little bit angry with Dad, for surely the sunshine did not make all that difference to the water.

"I think you're a big scaredy-cat, Dad," he burst out.

Dad did not like that. He made up his mind to show Bobby that he was not a scaredy-cat after all.

"Come on, then, Bobby," he cried, "I'll soon let you see. I'll race you to see who is in the water first."

Dad and Bobby both hurried as fast as they could to get their clothes off and their bathing trunks on. Dad was quicker than Bobby and so was ready first. Across the sand he ran, right to the water's edge—and there he came to a halt. Carefully he put his right foot forward and slid it into the water. "Oh!", he said, "that water's cold!" and he quickly drew his foot out again. Next he put his left foot forward and slowly slid it into the water. "Oh!," he said again, "the water *is* cold," and he quickly drew his foot back out.

Dad stood at the very edge of the water, trying to pluck up enough courage to go in. As he stood there shivering, Bobby came running over the sand to join his Dad. When Bobby came to the water's edge, *he* did not stop! No, he kept on running, splashing the water up in the air as he ran and did not stop until he had plunged headfirst into the sea. Then he turned to speak to Dad. "Come on, Dad," he said.

"Isn't the water a bit cold, Bobby?" replied Dad timidly.

"Yes, it *is* cold," agreed Bobby, "but it is great fun once you are in."

It was great fun once he was in! Bobby had discovered the secret of enjoying a bathe—to plunge in and not stand shivering on the shore. And that is the secret of enjoying life, too. Some people hang back from the service of Jesus because they think it is too hard, that he asks too much. Serving Jesus *is* hard and he *does* ask a lot—but it is "great fun once you are in!"

BOBBY LIKES 'THE HOLIDAYS'

Bobby is back at school again after the holidays. The week before he went back, his aunt and uncle came visiting.

"How are you enjoying school just now?" his aunt asked.

"I am enjoying it very well just now," Bobby replied. "It's super."

Bobby's aunt thought that was splendid and was very pleased.

Bobby's aunt and uncle came visiting again, and once again his aunt asked him how he was enjoying school.

"Bobby," she said, "are you enjoying school just as much as you were the last time I saw you? You said then that it was 'super'. Is it still as good?"

"No," said Bobby, "it's terrible now."

"I'm sorry to hear that," said his aunt. "What's happened, what is different from the last time I asked you?"

"The difference is that school has started up again after the holidays."

Bobby's aunt was a bit disappointed at this and she turned to Jimmy, Bobby's chum, who was in the house at the time.

"How do *you* like school, Jimmy?"

Jimmy replied, "I like it shut, same as Bobby."

Bobby's aunt said next, "What is it that you don't like about school?"

"I don't like the lessons," said Bobby, "but I do like the holidays."

Bobby does not like work. He wants it to be holidays all the time! But if school were all holidays and no work, nobody would ever learn anything, and school would do nobody any good. It does do good—especially if you have a good teacher.

Some people get very fed up with life, just as Bobby and Jimmy got fed up with school, simply because it is sometimes very hard. But life *is* worthwhile and worth working hard at—especially with a good teacher like Jesus.

WHEN BOBBY STARTED SCHOOL

Bobby was so glad when he was old enough to start school. He had been looking forward to it for a long time, and would have started long ago if he had been allowed. For weeks beforehand he could hardly talk about anything except going to school so when his first day came he was terribly excited. He was up and dressed at six o'clock in the morning and he thought the hands of the clock would never move round towards school time.

At last it came and off went Bobby with his shining new school bag (his bag was quite empty of course, but that did not matter so far as Bobby was concerned). Bobby's mum went with him, as mums often do when their boys and girls go to school for the first time. She took him to the school and left him there to start his lessons while she went away off home again. Bobby was as happy as he could be, but Mum was just a little bit sad. If Bobby had been there he might have seen a tear squeeze its way out of the corner of her eye and roll slowly down her cheek. That is the way mums often feel when their babies grow up to be such big boys and girls that they have to go to school!

The house seemed empty without Bobby in it and all morning his mum felt very lonely. At last, however, the morning was over and Bobby came rushing home. "Well, Bobby," said his mum, "did you like school?" "Oh, yes, Mum," said Bobby, "it was great fun."

Next morning Bobby was *not* up and dressed at six o'clock then. In fact, Bobby was still in bed when his mum came to his bedroom much later than that. "Come on, Bobby," she called, "you must get up now. It will soon be time for you to go to school." "It's all right,

Mum," Bobby replied, "I am not going to bother going to school today. I'll just stay at home and play. I might go back to school tomorrow." "You will get out of your bed this minute," his mum said firmly, "once you have started school you have got to keep going."

Poor Bobby! He thought he could go to school just when he felt like it, but the rest of us know better than that! We know that once you start school you must keep going all the time.

There are some people as silly as Bobby was. They seem to think that you can make a beginning in the service of Jesus and then just stop and start whenever you like.

There is a verse in the bible which tells us "not to grow weary in well-doing". Once we have enlisted in Jesus' service, we must keep going with all our might.

BOBBY IS DISAPPOINTED WITH SCHOOL

After Bobby had been going to school for nearly two weeks, he told his mum that he was disappointed with it. Long before he was school age he had looked forward to going to school and was very keen to get started. And all the first week he was at school he appeared to enjoy it very much. When he came home, he had always a lot to say about what he had been doing. But when it came to his second week, Bobby's mum began to wonder if he was as happy with school as he had been the first week. Oh, he never made any fuss about going, once he understood he had to go each day, but each day he seemed to have less and less to say about it. In fact he seemed to come home from school as if a big black cloud was resting on his head. He went to school every morning bright and cheery, but he always came home from school 'down-in-the-mouth'.

This went on every day that week and never got any better. Mum became more and more worried every day and, when Bobby came home on Friday downcast and depressed again, she could stand it no longer.

"Bobby," she said, "what is wrong with you?"

"Nothing," said Bobby.

But Bobby's mum was determined to get to the bottom of the mystery and she said to him, "Come now, Bobby, there is something that has upset you. Is it to do with school?"

"Yes," admitted Bobby, "I am very disappointed with school."

"You are disappointed with school?" replied Mum. "Why are you disappointed?"

"Well," came Bobby's answer, "I have been going there for two whole weeks and I still can't read and I still can't write!"

That, of course, was rather a silly thing to say. Imagine thinking that school was a failure because he had not learned to read or write in only two weeks!

Yet some of us at times can be just as foolish as Bobby, not with regard to school but with regard to Jesus. The Bible tells us that Jesus can make us better boys and girls, and better men and women, if only we make up our minds to follow him. Sometimes we may get disappointed because Jesus does not make us perfect all at once.

It was not the fault of the school that Bobby did not learn to read and write in two weeks. I suppose his teacher could have taught him to read and write in that time, if Bobby had been able to take in as quickly as that. But a little boy was not able to learn all that in such a short time.

In a similar way, Jesus has to work with us as we are. He is able to improve us, but usually only a little at a time. If however we keep trusting him and keep trying to obey him, he will make us better and better.

BOBBY HAS A 'TEST'

Bobby is now in his second year at school. That means that he is no longer one of the 'babies' of the school; and he is very proud of that fact! When school opened for the session, Bobby felt that he was grown up as he watched all the beginners being brought along by their mums. "I am glad," he said to himself, "that I am a big boy now. I would not like to be just an infant starting school for the first time. It is grand to be in my second year and no longer a beginner."

Bobby soon found out however that being in the second year had its snags as well. He came home at lunch-time one day last week in a dreadful state. Mum did not take long to discover that something was wrong, for Bobby refused a second helping of pudding and that was something he never did—unless he was sick. "Are you feeling all right, Bobby?" Mum asked anxiously.

"Yes," replied Bobby, "I am all right, but I am worried. Teacher is going to give us a test and I have never had a test before. I don't know what a test is like, and I don't think I will be able to do it."

Mum tried to cheer Bobby up and get him to stop worrying but it was no good. He was upset over the test due in the afternoon and, if Mum had allowed him, he would have stayed at home instead of going back to school. Mum, however, would not let him stay at home, so off he went with a face so worried-looking that it made Mum's heart quite sad to see it.

By this time Mum was just as worried about Bobby as Bobby was about the test. The time seemed to drag past as she waited anxiously for him to get back from school. At last he arrived—and came into the house as bright and happy as ever.

"Oh, Bobby," said Mum, "how did you get on with your test this afternoon?"

"We didn't get any test in the afternoon," answered Bobby, "we'd had it in the morning all the time! It was just ordinary things like spelling and reading and sums."

Bobby was so worried about his test, but it had already taken place and, in any case, it was just doing ordinary things.

Life too has its tests, tests of our goodness and our courage and our strength. But often these tests are really ordinary, everyday things and if we remember that Jesus goes with us wherever we go, we do not need to fear anything.

BOBBY AND THE SCHOOL PHOTOGRAPH

Bobby had his photograph taken at school the other day. It was not just a photograph of himself. It was a photograph of the whole class. His teacher told the class the day before that the photographer was coming to take a group photograph of all of them together and their mums would be able to buy copies of it if they wanted to do so.

Bobby was very excited about this and told Mum about it as soon as he arrived home.

"I'll have to look my best, won't I, Mum?" he said.

"You will indeed, Bobby," was the reply, "but don't worry, I'll see that you go to school perfectly clean and as smart as is possible. It will be up to you to keep yourself that way for the photograph, and to smile nicely when the photographer takes his pictures."

The following morning Mum was as good as her word. Bobby went away to school looking just great. His clothes were smart and neat, and even his tie was straight! His hands were spotlessly clean and his face was shining. His hair was nicely brushed and he looked just perfect.

When Bobby came home from school, the first thing Mum said to him was, "Well, how did the class photograph go?"

"Fine," Bobby answered, "it went fine, I kept myself

clean and I kept my tie straight and I remembered to smile when the photogaph was being taken."

"That was good," said Mum, "and when will you get the photographs?"

"We have to take the money for it tomorrow and we will get the photograph next Wednesday."

When next Wednesday came, Bobby went off to school even more excited than he had been the day the photograph was taken. But when he came home, he was very quiet and looked a bit disappointed.

"What's wrong, Bobby?" Mum asked. "Did you not get your photograph after all?"

"Yes, I got it all right, but I don't like it. It's not very good."

"That's a pity," said Mum, "let me see it." Bobby handed her the photograph.

"Why, Bobby," Mum said, "I think it's a very good photograph. I don't know why you are disappointed with it."

"Well," said Bobby, "I agree that it is very good of everybody else, but it's not good of me. I'm really much better-looking than I am in the photograph."

The truth is that it was a very good photograph of Bobby as well as of everybody else. It was really very like him. Bobby just did not recognise it as a good likeness. Or rather, Bobby failed to see himself as he really is. But

Bobby is not alone in that. Lots of us fail to see ourselves as we really are. Lots of us imagine that we are a lot better than we really are. Other people can often see us more clearly than we see ourselves.

God sees us clearly. He sees all our faults and failings. But the wonder is that He still loves us, despite knowing all our faults.

BOBBY HAS CHICKEN-POX

Bobby is absent from school. He went off at the beginning of last week and will be off for a bit yet. He has chicken-pox. But you need not feel sorry for him, because Bobby is not feeling at all sorry for himself. He is not seriously ill and, to tell you the truth, he is really quite pleased that he has developed chicken-pox.

In fact, Bobby was quite worried because he thought he was going to miss it! Chicken-pox has been going the rounds in Bobby's school class for a number of weeks now and one by one the children have been absent. But Bobby kept on being so healthy that he began to be afraid that the chicken-pox was going to pass him by. Then a fortnight or so ago the boy who sat next to Bobby in the class caught it, and Bobby became more anxious than ever! He started to examine himself all over every morning as soon as he was awake to see if there were any spots, but each morning he just had to trot away to school, spot-free!

On the Tuesday morning, Bobby rushed up to his father's bedside, shouting loudly, "They're here, they're here!" Bobby's father got rather a fright at first. It was only seven o'clock in the morning, after all, and poor Dad had been fast asleep. "Who's here?" he cried out in alarm, "who's here?" "The spots," said Bobby, "my spots have come at last. I think I've got chicken-pox!"

And so he had, for when the doctor came he looked at Bobby's spots and said right away that it was chicken-pox and that Bobby must stay off school.

Don't feel too sorry for Bobby, because Bobby is not feeling in the least sorry for himself. But do remember *how* Bobby got chicken-pox. *He caught it from the boy who sat beside him.*

We catch habits from the company we keep. That is why it matters so much that we should choose good company and not bad, and especially that we should choose the company of Jesus.

BOBBY TOUCHES 'WET PAINT'

Bobby came into the house the other day holding his hands behind his back and Mum knew right away that he was trying to hide something from her. In any case she could tell from his face that he was expecting trouble.

"What have you got there, Bobby?" she demanded.

"Nothing," was Bobby's answer.

"Come on now, Bobby, I know you better than that. Let me see what you are hiding behind your back," Mum said.

Bobby slowly brought his hands out where his mother could see them.

"Bobby," she said sharply, "how did you get your hands into such a mess?" The palms of Bobby's hands were all green paint.

This is how it happened. Bobby was strolling home from school, taking his time and looking around him, because it was a nice day and there is always something interesting to see if you look for it. As he went along the street, he came to a garden gate painted bright green with a notice beside it that said 'Wet Paint'.

Bobby stopped and looked at it and admired the brightness of the fresh paint. "I wonder if it is still wet?" he said to himself. "It looks dry to me, I'll touch it and see." Without thinking any more about it, he grabbed hold of the garden gate with both hands. The paint *was* still wet.

Bobby would not take a warning. He wanted to try the paint out for himself and so he got into a mess. Lots of people get themselves into trouble because they will not take a warning but insist on trying out wrong things for themselves.

There are, on the other hand, a lot of good things

which we will not know how good they are until we try them out for ourselves. Bobby, for instance, never used to take soup. He did not think he would like it, although he had never tried it. Then one day Mum persuaded him to taste some and he found that he liked it after all. Now it is one of his favourite dishes.

It can be like that with many things. We do not find out how good they are until we try them for ourselves. That is certainly the case with Christianity. Jesus says that we will not find the best in life until we take him as our Leader and our Friend. How true that is.

BOBBY IS IMPORTANT

One day at school Bobby's teacher was speaking to the class about some of the marvellous new things that had come into the world this century. She was telling them how men and women had invented so many things that people of older times knew nothing about.

After she had been talking to them for a time, she started to ask the boys and girls in turn to name one of these modern treasures. "Tell me," she said to each of them, one after another, "tell me something important that was not in the world before this century."

Different answers came:

Motor cars
Washing machines
Television
Aeroplanes
Potato Crisps

*Telephones
and so on*

When it came to Bobby's turn, nearly all the things he had thought of had already been mentioned and he could not think what to say. His teacher tried to encourage him. "Can you think of any important thing that is in the world today that was not there a hundred years ago?"

Bobby thought just a moment longer, and then he said, "Please, miss — me."

The rest of the class burst out laughing, and even Teacher smiled. But although that was not the answer she was looking for, Bobby's answer was true.

Bobby is important. He matters to his mum and dad and little sister and to all the other people who know him and love him. And he matters to God. He is very important to God, as we all are, every one of us.

Jesus made that very plain. For example, he told a story once about a shepherd who had exactly one hundred sheep, and one day one of them was lost. Some people said, "Why worry? You've got ninety-nine left, that's enough." But the shepherd replied, "No, I love that lost sheep, too. It matters to me." And he went and braved all sorts of dangers to search and search until he found his lost sheep and brought it back.

Jesus told that story to show that just as one sheep mattered to the shepherd, so every one of us matters to God. He loves us all.

BOBBY IS NEVER AFRAID IF DAD IS THERE

Bobby is a member of the Boys' Brigade. He is in the section for very young boys—the Anchor Boys' Section—and it meets on a Friday evening in the church hall. He enjoys it very much and enjoys talking about it, too.

He was telling one of his school friends about it the other day, and his friend said, "But isn't it dark by the time the meeting is finished and you go home?"

"Yes," said Bobby. "it *is* dark by then."

"Oh," his friend replied, "I would not like that. I would be frightened coming home in the dark. Aren't you frightened, Bobby?"

"No," Bobby said, rather scornfully, "I'm not frightened."

"Aren't you just a little bit frightened? That's a very dark stretch just before you come to your street. Aren't you frightened even there?"

"No," Bobby said again, "I'm not frightened. I'm not frightened anywhere on the way home."

Bobby's friend's eyes were almost popping out with admiration by this time. "That's really wonderful," he said. "You must be very brave. How do you do it?"

"Well, you see," Bobby explained, "my dad always comes and meets me at the church hall door. I walk home with him all the way and I am never afraid when my dad is with me."

It can make such a difference to have someone we love and trust with us in dark and stormy times.

To have Jesus as our Friend means that we have him with us all the time. What a difference that can make! We cannot see Jesus beside us, but he *is* there. What is more, he has promised that he will *always* be beside his friends, wherever they have to go.

Bible Sunday

BOBBY WANTS A BIGGER BIBLE

Bobby has a Bible of his own and he is very proud of it. He takes it with him to church every Sunday, and he looks up the passage when the minister comes to the Bible-reading part of the service. He tries to follow the lesson in his Bible as it is being read, but sometimes he finds it too difficult to keep up with the minister.

Bobby is still quite a slow reader, especially when he comes to big words, and often the minister reads too fast for him. He likes it better when he is reading his Bible at home by himself for then he can take his time. He can even stop to think about what he has been reading.

The other day Bobby said to Mum, "I would like to have a new Bible."

"Why?" asked Mum, "what's wrong with the one you've got? It looks all right to me."

"It is all right," replied Bobby, "but I would like a bigger one. I see other people at the church with much bigger Bibles than mine. I think a bigger one must be better."

"Why do you think a bigger Bible must be a better Bible?" Mum asked him.

"Well," Bobby replied, "if it's bigger there must be more in it, mustn't there, and therefore it must be better."

"That's just where you're wrong, Bobby," his mother said. "Bigger Bibles don't have any more in them than smaller Bibles have. It is just that the size of the *print* is bigger. Even the smallest Bible has the same number of books and all the same stories as the biggest Bible in the world. And so has your Bible. It's got the same sixty-six books in it as are in the giant Bible that the minister has in the pulpit. Your ordinary-sized Bible is every bit as important as a much bigger one would be, because it contains the very same marvellous stories of God and Jesus and their love for us."

Bobby felt much happier about his Bible after Mum had explained this to him. He decided that he would keep it after all rather than get a bigger one.

"I realise now, in any case," he said to himself, "that it is not the size of anything that decides what it is worth. After all, a real gold ring is worth far more than a cheap bangle ten times its size."

When Bobby starts to think and talk to himself like this, he sometimes goes on and on. That is just what he did here. "No," he said to himself again, "size is not always the most important thing. Just as well, too, for no one would want little boys and girls if size was all that counted. Everybody would want baby elephants instead."

Then Bobby had another thought. "It's a jolly good job," he said to himself, "that our size is not what matters to God. He loves all of us just the same, whether we are big or small. My Bible tells me that."

BOBBY FALLS OUT OF BED

Bobby's bedroom is upstairs. His mum and dad used sometimes to heave sighs of relief when they got him settled down for the night, especially if they had had a boisterous sort of day with him. Once they had tucked him up, heard him say his prayers and said goodnight, they found it lovely and peaceful and relaxing to sit quietly in the living room below with the paper, a magazine or book, or just watch television.

For the last week or so, however, once they have seen Bobby into bed they have not been able to relax one little bit. The trouble is that Bobby started to fall out of bed.

The first time it happened they did not know what is was and got a dreadful fright. They had said their goodnights to Bobby just as usual and were settled down in their armchairs in the room below when, suddenly, there was an almighty 'thump' just above their heads.

They leaped to their feet and rushed up the stairs,

wondering if the roof had fallen in. When they went into Bobby's room, they found the answer right away. There was Bobby lying flat on his back beside his bed and he was fast asleep. He had fallen out of bed with that thump and it had not even wakened him up!

Dad picked him up, put him back into bed and covered him up. Then they went back downstairs again, a bit upset and asking each other if it was likely to happen again. They found it difficult to settle down and could not concentrate at first on what they were doing. But all was well and they did not hear another sound from Bobby's room that night.

The next night, however, the very same thing happened. They had seen Bobby safely off to bed and to sleep, and were sitting peacefully in their chairs down below. Then, suddenly, 'thump', and this time they knew what it was before they got to Bobby's bedroom. Sure enough, there he was lying on the bedside rug once more. This time, however, the fall had woken him up.

"What's happened?" he asked.

"You've fallen out of bed," said Mum. "Are you all right?"

"Yes, I'm fine," replied Bobby, and so they tucked him up in bed once more.

The following night it happened again, Bobby in bed, goodnight said, Mum and Dad downstairs, a period of quiet and then 'thump'—and Bobby was on the floor again.

When they picked him up once more and put him back

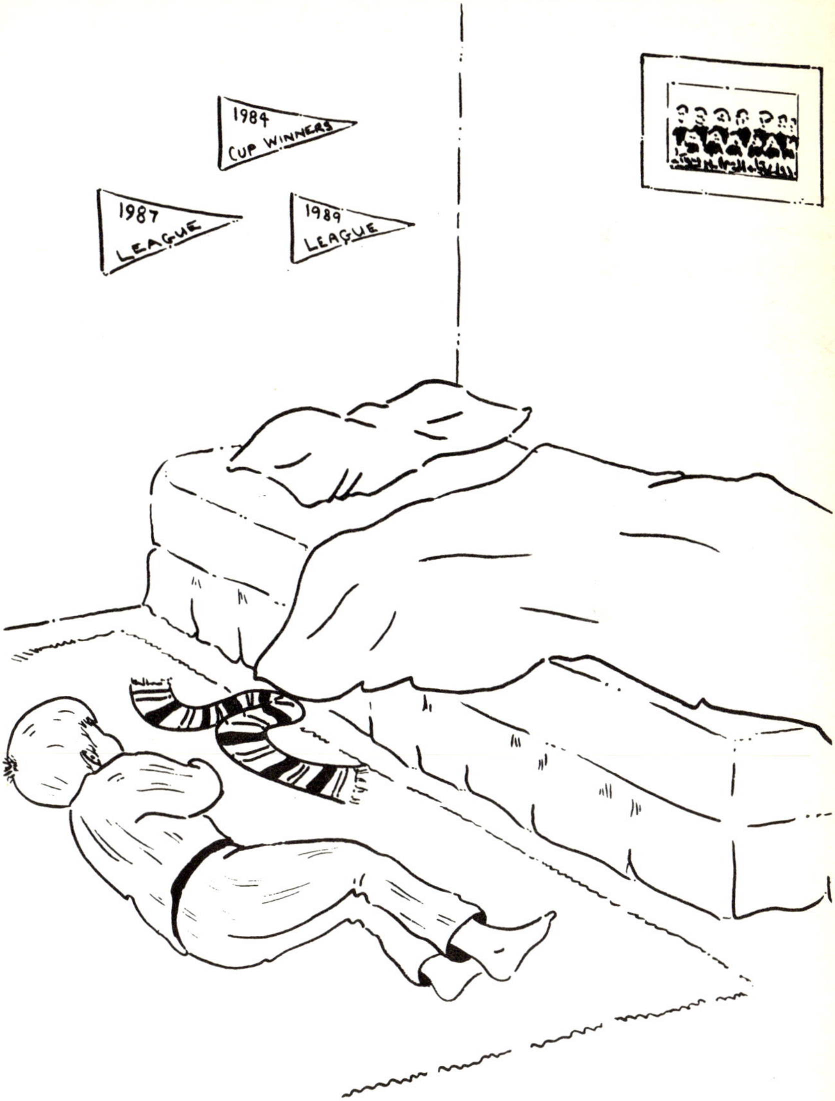
1984
CUP WINNERS
1987
LEAGUE
1989
LEAGUE

into bed, Mum said, "I wonder, Bobby, why you keep falling out of bed like this?"

"I think," Bobby said, "it may be because I go to sleep too near the place where I get in. I'm going to crawl over to the middle of the bed before I close my eyes in future."

And it has worked. He has not fallen out of bed again since, and his Mum and Dad can relax in the evening once more. The trouble probably was that, as he put it, Bobby was going to sleep too "near the place where he got in".

That is often the trouble with many of us in other ways. We enter into something good and worthwhile, but we soon become tired of it. We fall asleep too near the place where we get in.

Sometimes it can be like that with following Jesus, but the Bible has plenty of encouragement for us to attempt to finish what we begin.

BOBBY'S DIRTY HANDS

It was Saturday morning and Bobby was spending it outside. All morning he had been out in the garden playing. He was pretending that he was at the seaside and building castles on the sand. He had dug a hole in the corner of the garden where his dad allowed him to play. After that he had filled up the hole with water and he was now building a castle out of the mud that the water had made in the hole. It was terribly dirty work and Bobby enjoyed every minute of it!

He was busily occupied in the very tricky task of constructing the castle's drawbridge when suddenly there was a knock on the window and Mum called, "Lunch is ready, Bobby." Bobby had not realised it was so late. The time had seemed to pass so quickly. He did not answer Mum, but he kept on making his drawbridge, pressing the mud into shape with his hands. His lunch would just have to wait. It was important work on which he was engaged, and an everyday thing like food must not be allowed to interfere with it.

"Bobby, come for your lunch," Mum called again. "All right," Bobby called back — and carried on making his drawbridge. Then he heard the sound of the door opening and Mum calling out "Bobby!" much more sharply than before and Bobby knew that it was now time to move.

He left his castle and rushed inside. When Mum saw him she gave a gasp and exclaimed, "Bobby, however did you get your hands into such a state? They are positively filthy. Get them scrubbed clean at once before you dare come near the table."

Bobby did not think there was much wrong with his hands the way they were, but he did not argue. Off he trotted to the hand-basin. He picked up the sponge, pressed it against the soap and then began to rub it up and down the palms of his hands. When he had finished, he dried his hands and went into the dining-room. "Let me see your hands before you sit down," said Mum. Bobby held up his hands with the palms facing outwards. "That is much better," said Mum. "Take your place at the table."

They all sat down, grace was said, and Bobby reached out his hand to pick up his soup spoon.

"Bobby," cried Mum, "your hands won't do at all! They are clean only on one side. Go and wash the other sides at once." Bobby had to make his way back to the hand-basin to finish washing his dirty hands. As he did so, he grumbled, "Mum expects far too much. I shouldn't need to wash both sides every time I wash my hands."

Do *you* think Mum was asking too much of Bobby? Of course not. Yet some people seem to think that if they keep the outside of their lives clean, it does not matter whether the inside is clean or not. Jesus says that these are foolish people, for being clean inside — in our heart and mind and soul — is the most important thing.

BOBBY AND THE BLACKBIRD'S NEST

There is a nest in a corner of Bobby's garden. In that corner there is a bush and recently blackbirds began to build there. All day long they could be seen flying out from the bush and then back in again, carrying wisps of straw and things like that in their beaks. Two or three days later the nest was completed. The day after the nest was finished, Bobby saw the mother blackbird sitting on the nest. She sat there for ages and ages and ages. When she finally flew away, she left a lovely speckled egg lying in the nest.

The next day the same thing happened. Mother blackbird sat on the nest for ages and ages and ages and, when she flew away, there were now two eggs lying side by side in the nest. The next day she laid a third egg, and the following day she laid a fourth egg. The next day she laid a fifth egg, but after that she did not lay any more.

Then she and father blackbird began to take it in turns to sit on the eggs to keep them warm and so hatch them out. There was hardly any time when one of the blackbirds was not sitting on the eggs. This went on for a number of days and then one by one the eggs cracked open and the little baby blackbirds were hatched out.

So now there was a family of five tiny blackbirds in the nest in the bush in the corner of Bobby's garden. Bobby was very excited when he saw them. The nest was just too high up for Bobby to see it by himself, but every day his Dad lifted him up to look in at some moment when father and mother blackbird were not there.

When Dad lifted him up to see the newly hatched-out babies, Bobby was very excited indeed. He had never seen such young birds before. How funny they looked, so tiny, with no feathers, their eyes shut and their beaks open.

"Dad," said Bobby, "can I get these baby birds out of the nest to play with me?"

"Oh, no!" Dad replied, "if you did that, it would kill them."

"But I would not hurt them, Dad," pleaded Bobby. "I just want to play with them for a little while and then put them back."

"No, Bobby", said his dad, "I know that you do not want to hurt them, but if we take these little birds out of their nest, I assure you that they will die. And remember, Bobby"—he said this in a louder voice—"don't you dare try to take any of them out yourself when I'm not here." (Although Bobby was not tall enough to see into the nest, he was tall enough to be able to reach it with his hand when he stood on tiptoe and stretched up as far as he could.)

Bobby's dad went into the house just then and Bobby was left in the garden all by himself. As soon as he realised he was alone, Bobby said to himself: "I am sure it would not do any harm if I lifted one of the baby birds out for a minute before their mother comes back to the nest." So he looked to the right and he looked to the left to see that no one was looking and then, standing up on tiptoe, he began to stretch his hand slowly up towards the nest.

"Bobby!" his dad's voice shouted, "what did I tell you? Leave that nest *alone*!"

Bobby got such a fright that his heart nearly popped out of his mouth. He dropped his hand at once, and jumped round to see where the voice was coming from. And there was his dad at the bedroom window upstairs. He had gone to change and, happening to look out of the window, had seen Bobby up to his tricks.

Poor Bobby! He thought there was no-one to see him doing wrong, but his dad was watching him all the time. Of course, even if his dad had not seen him, there would still have been Someone who would have known what Bobby was doing!

Perhaps you and I are sometimes tempted to try and do

a wrong thing secretly, thinking that no-one can see us and hoping that no-one will find us out. We should remember that, even if no-one else knows what we are doing, God does.

BOBBY AND A MISUNDERSTANDING

It was Bobby's first day in the Primary Department of his Sunday School. He was five now and he had been promoted from the Beginners' to the Primary Department. Bobby was very proud of his step up. He felt that he was no longer an infant, but was beginning to be quite grown up. Bobby was therefore quite excited as he went along to the Primary for the first time. Up to the church hall he went, through the door, up the stairs and along the passage to the hall where the Primary met, pushed open the door—and, oh dear, he was late. The Primary had already started and Bobby did not know where to sit. But the Leader of the Primary was very kind and, as soon as she saw Bobby, she said, "I am glad that you have managed to come, Bobby. I will put you into your proper class later. Will you just wait here for the present?"—and she put Bobby into a seat in the front row.

At first Bobby seemed to be enjoying the Primary Department very much, but if you had been watching his face, you would have noticed it grow longer and longer as the time went past, and by the end he looked very glum. "Good afternoon, Bobby," said the Leader as he went out of the door. "I hope you enjoyed today and I will look forward to seeing you again next Sunday." Bobby just gave a grunt.

He had more to say, however, when he reached home. "I don't think I will go back to the Primary," he announced.

"You don't think you'll go back?" said Mum. "Why, did you not like it?"

"I liked it all right," replied Bobby, "but I don't think I will go back all the same. The Leader tells lies."

"Oh, Bobby," said Mum, "I am sure the Leader does not tell lies. You must be making a mistake."

"Well, she told me a lie anyway," Bobby answered, "so I don't think I will go back."

"She told you a lie?" Mum said. "What was the lie she told you?"

"Well," said Bobby, "when I went in, she gave me a seat and told me to wait there for the present—and I haven't got the present yet."

Poor Bobby! He had completely misunderstood the Leader's words. She meant, of course, that he was to wait there "for just now", but Bobby thought she meant he was to receive a gift. Mum was soon able to explain it all to Bobby and that put matters right.

Bobby is not the only person who misunderstands words. Lots of people do. Sometimes they misunderstand important words. Worst of all, sometimes people misunderstand the words of Jesus which are the most important words in the whole world.

For instance, Jesus once said, "Suffer the little children

to come unto me." Some people seem to think these words mean "Let children come to me if they want, although I would rather not be bothered with them." They really mean, "Encourage the children to come to me, for I love them all."

Baptismal Sunday

BOBBY VISITS A NEW BABY

Bobby sometimes does things or says things in public that make his mum feel very embarrassed. When she took him with her to see a brand new baby, this is just what happened and she wished a hole would open up in the floor so that she could drop right into it and hide her face.

One of Mum's friends has just had a baby and she wanted to visit her and see the baby. She thought Bobby and Susan would enjoy seeing the baby too, so she took them with her.

When they got there, the baby was lying sleeping in his cot. It was a baby boy and he was lovely (as every baby is) and they all had a good look at him.

"Isn't he just gorgeous?" said Mum, all smiles.

"He's wonderful," said Susan, her eyes dancing with pleasure. "I wish we could take him home with us."

Bobby said nothing to begin with and, truth to tell, he did not look very excited.

"Well, then, Bobby," Mum said to him, "what do you

think of the new baby? Isn't he lovely?"

"Oh, he's all right," Bobby replied in a matter-of-fact way. "He's all right, but I've seen babies before. They're really all the same, aren't they? One is no different from any other."

Bobby's Mum was *so* embarrassed. What a thing to say in front of the baby's mother! She, of course, thought her baby was the most beautiful in all the world and not at all like any other baby.

And so indeed he was. Bobby was quite wrong in thinking that babies are all the same. They are in fact all different. Every baby is an individual person. Every mother knows that. And God knows that, too.

We are not just numbers to God. He knows and loves us as individuals.

BOBBY'S POCKET

Bobby trouser pockets are like some ladies' handbags — packed full to bursting! One night when he was getting undressed for his bath before going to bed, Mum said to him, "Bobby, what on earth have you got in your trouser pockets? You'll spoil them, cramming them so full."

"Oh," said Bobby, "just one or two things, not very much."

"Just one or two things?" said Mum. "We'll have just a look, shall we?" And before Bobby could say another word, she began to empty out the first pocket. You would hardly believe that one trouser pocket could hold all the things that came out of that one.

Here is a list of its contents:

1 Broken Pencil
2 Pieces of String
3 Pebbles of different sizes
1 Pocket-knife with a broken blade
1 Caramel toffee wrapped in paper (a bit dirty)
1 Caramel toffee not wrapped in paper (a bit dirtier)
1 Christmas party paper hat
1 Whistle
1 Broken piece of shoe-lace
3 Badges
1 Toy motor lorry with only two wheels
1 Water Pistol

When she saw all that had come out of one pocket, Mum said to Bobby, "What a load of rubbish! Why do you keep such things in your pocket?"

"Because they belong to me and I love them all," replied Bobby.

The things in Bobby's pocket maybe did not look very nice, but they were all important to him. The world contains a lot of very different people and some of them may not look very nice. But they all belong to God and He loves every one of them. That means, of course, that He loves us, too.

BOBBY THINKS THAT SUSAN DOESN'T COUNT

Bobby and his little sister, Susan, had been invited to a birthday party in their friend's house. They were very pleased and excited about it. When the day of the party came they became even more excited. Mum got them washed and then dressed in their party clothes, and they were ready to be taken to their friend's home.

Before they left their own house, Mum said to them, "I want you both to be on your best behaviour at the party, and I want *you,* Bobby, to be sure to be polite and nice to all the girls. Give everyone a turn at the games. Don't leave any of them out."

Later on when it was time for the end of the party, Mum went back and collected Bobby and Susan.

"Was it a good party?" she asked.

"Oh, yes," replied Bobby, "it was smashing. There was lovely food and lots of lovely games."

"And," said Mum, "did you remember what I said about being polite and giving every girl a turn with you when you were playing the games?"

"Yes," Bobby answered, "I remembered and I did it. I made sure I gave every girl a turn with me."

"No, you didn't," Susan called out, "you never gave me a turn. You never played with me once during the whole party."

"Oh," said Bobby, "I didn't think you counted since you are my sister."

Bobby was wrong to think that his little sister didn't count. But that's the kind of mistake lots of us make at times. We forget about the people who are nearest to us. We sometimes think they do not really matter. But, of course, they do.

One marvellous thing that Jesus made plain for us is that every single one of us matters to God. He never forgets any of us, at any time.

BOBBY FINDS A RIDDLE

Bobby is very fond of riddles and he is always trying to catch me out with them. He used to catch me nearly every time but I have bought one or two books of riddles so that I might be able to answer some of Bobby's riddles. Last week I knew the answer to every one he asked me.

"Can you tell me," he said, "why the fireman wore red braces?"

"Yes," I replied, "it was to keep his trousers up."

Bobby was surprised that I knew the answer, but he was even more surprised when I was able to answer three more riddles. Here they are:

"What is the best thing to put into a pie?"
 "Your teeth."
"What will happen if you drop a white hat into the Red Sea?"
 "It will get wet."

"Why did the boy put ice in his father's bed?"
"Because he liked cold pop."

Bobby was not only surprised that I knew the answers to these riddles, but I could see that he was also a bit disappointed. So I said to him, "I tell you what, Bobby, if you can give me a riddle and I *can't* give you the answer, I will give you 10p."

"Right you are," said Bobby, and he thought and thought. Then he said, "How can you divide three apples between four children, so that every child gets a whole apple?"

Now it was my turn to think and think, but in the end I had to say, "I give in. Here's your 10p. Now tell me the answer."

Bobby put the 10p in his pocket and said, "I don't know the answer either. I don't even know if there is an answer. You never said anything about having to give you an answer as well as a question."

Fancy asking me a riddle which has no answer! But, you know, people sometimes ask impossible questions of the Christian faith, and then say, "The Christian faith cannot give me an answer, therefore it is no good." Jesus does not try to give us the answer to every question. He does assure us that God loves us.

BOBBY MAKES A SNOWMAN

When Bobby woke up one Saturday morning and looked through the window, his heart leaped for joy. It was a glorious day — at least, in Bobby's opinion it was a glorious day. The ground was white with a thick carpet of snow and the snow was still falling fast. "Goody!" cried Bobby with glee, and leaped quickly out of bed. He wasted no time in getting dressed and hurrying through his breakfast.

"Mum," he asked, "may I go out to play?"

"Not just now," Mum replied, "it is still snowing. Wait till it stops."

"Mum," said Bobby, five minutes later, "may I go out now?"

"No," answered Mum, "it is still snowing quite hard."

But after Bobby had made the same request for the eighth time, Mum said, "Oh, all right, so long as you are properly wrapped up." Bobby pulled on his thick jersey, his waterproof, his scarf, his cap, his Wellington boots and out he went.

It was marvellous. To begin with, Bobby was quite content to walk through the snow making lovely big footprints as he went. After that he began to make snowballs and throw them at the wall. They made such a lovely 'plop' when they landed. Then he thought it would be a good idea to throw snowballs not just at a wall, but at somebody. So he made a great big pile of snowballs and waited for someone to come along.

The first person to come was the postman. When Bobby

saw him coming, he hid behind the hedge and as the postman came up the path Bobby threw a snowball. I do not know whether Bobby was a very good 'aimer', or if he was just very lucky, but his snowball hit the postman right on the back of the head. How Bobby laughed! He did not laugh quite so much, I must say, when the postman picked up a handful of snow and stuffed it down the back of Bobby's neck.

Then Bobby thought it would be a good idea to make a snowman. There is a large open space of ground near where Bobby lives and he decided to make his snowman there. There was much more snow there than on his own front garden.

So round he plodded to the open space and set to work. He worked hard and he worked well, and in scarcely any time at all he had his snowman finished. He was a very handsome snowman indeed, and Bobby decided to call him 'Sammy'.

"You look very nice, Sammy," said Bobby, "but I think you will look even nicer with a cap on. It will keep your head warm, too. I don't want you to catch a cold."

Bobby ran off home to get an old cap for Sammy to wear. He was back two or three minutes later with the cap in his hand only to find that someone had stolen his snowman. Standing beside Sammy was a big boy, a bully, and when Bobby went to put the cap on Sammy's head this big bully said, "Here, keep off, you. This is my snowman."

"No, it's not," said Bobby, "it's mine. I made him."

"I don't care," said the bully, "he's mine now and I'm keeping him."

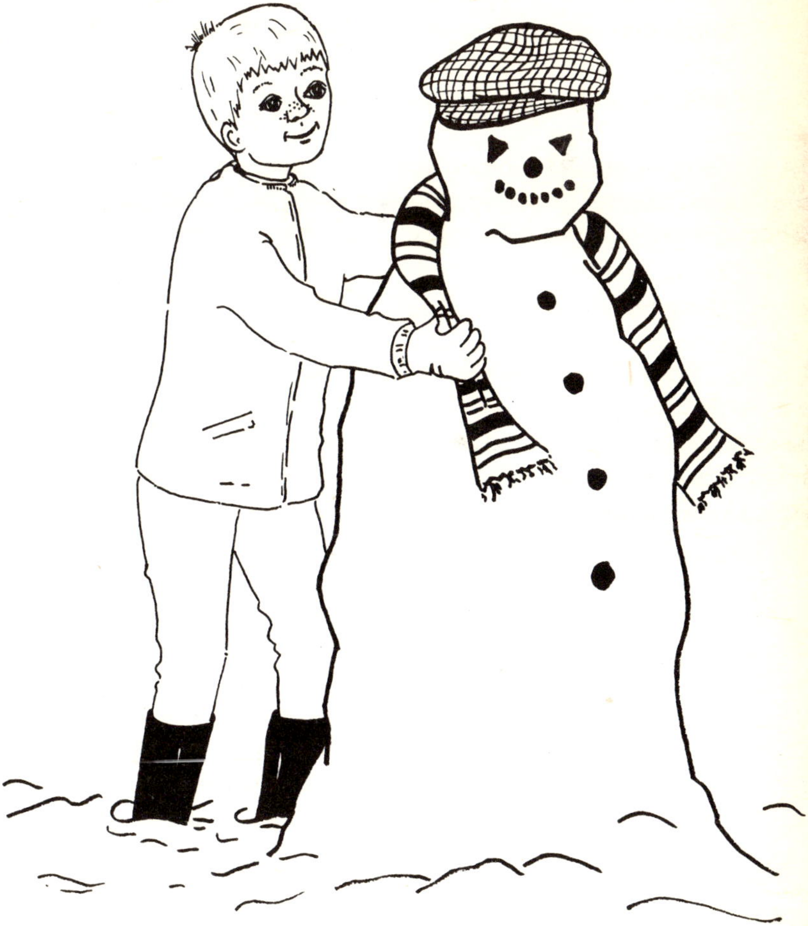

"I want him back," said Bobby, "you must give him back."

"No," said the bully, "I won't give him to you — but I tell you what, I'll sell him to you."

"But I've no money," said Bobby.

"Well, what do you have?" asked the bully.

Bobby thought for a moment and then he burst out, "I've a big heap of snowballs in my front garden. I'll buy back my snowman with those if you like."

"All right," said the bully. So Bobby carried round his snowballs — there must have been more than twenty — and the bully went away with them leaving Sammy to Bobby.

Bobby put the cap on the snowman and put his arm round it. "I love you, Sammy," he said, "and now you are really mine. In fact, you are twice mine, for I made you and now I've bought you."

Jesus could speak to us in the same way. We are twice his, for he has made us and he has bought us. To begin with, he made us, giving us the gift of life, and then he bought us, bought us back from the grip of sin at the cost of his own life. But of course we become really his only when we decide to accept him as our Saviour and Friend.

BOBBY GIVES SANTA CLAUS A KISS

Bobby had a great time at his Sunday School Christmas party. He had been looking forward to it for weeks and when it came it was wonderful. First of all the children had their tea and Bobby ate and ate. I could not tell you just how many sandwiches and cakes he had, but when one of the teachers asked him if he had had enough to eat, he replied, "Oh, yes. In fact, I think I would burst if I ate any more!"

At that moment another teacher came along carrying a plate of cakes. "Would you like another cake, Bobby?" she asked.

"Yes, please," said Bobby.

"I thought you said you might burst if you ate any more," remarked the first teacher.

"Oh, well," said Bobby, "I think I will take the risk but perhaps you should stand back just in case."

After tea the children played games — and then, suddenly, there was the sound of tinkling bells, a loud knocking on the door and in came Santa Claus with a huge sack of toys on his back. In his sack there was a present for every boy and girl in the room. Bobby got a space-ship.

After all the children had received their gifts, Santa picked up his sack and prepared to leave. Suddenly Bobby ran over to him again. Santa bent down and said, "Yes, Bobby, what is it?"

"It has been a lovely party, Santa," said Bobby, "you have given me a lovely present and I want to say 'thank you'. I would like to give you a present but since I have not anything else, I will give you this" — and he gave Santa a kiss on each cheek.

That was a lovely thing that Bobby did, for it is always good to say 'thank you' — especially at Christmas time.

It is because of God and God's love that we have Christmas and parties and presents. It is all because, at the first Christmas, God gave us Jesus to be our Friend and our Saviour. We may feel, as Bobby felt, that we have not much to give to show our thanks. But we can give God our hearts and our love — and that is really what he would like best.

What can I give Him,
Poor as I am?
If I were a shepherd
I would bring a lamb;
If I were a wise man,
I would do my part
Yet what I can I give him —
Give my heart.

(Christina Rossetti)

BOBBY AND THE TOY SANTA

Bobby does not like going to bed at night, and Mum usually has quite a hard job getting him upstairs when bedtime comes. But on Christmas Eve she got a surprise. As soon as ever he had finished his evening meal, Bobby said, "I want to go to bed."

Mum was worried. "Are you feeling ill, Bobby?" she asked.

"No, I'm all right. I just want to go to bed."

"But why do you want to go to bed so early as this if you are feeling all right?"

"Well, Mum," Bobby explained patiently, "this is the night that Santa Claus comes, and the quicker I get to sleep the quicker it will be morning."

So off he went to bed although it was only six o'clock. He did not even want to read, or shout and sing, as he sometimes does after going to bed. He lay down right away to go to sleep. At seven o'clock when everything had been very quiet for about an hour, Mum tip-toed upstairs to see that Bobby was all right. Quietly she poked her head round the door and at once a voice said, "Is that you Santa Claus?" "No," replied Mum, "it's only seven o'clock."

"Oh dear," said Bobby, "I can't get to sleep." He must have been very excited, because he took a long time to fall asleep. At eight o'clock he was downstairs for a glass of milk; at nine o'clock he came down for a biscuit and at ten o'clock he appeared to ask what time it was. When Dad went away to the Christmas Eve Service about eleven o'clock, Bobby was still awake; but when Dad came back about half-past twelve, Bobby was fast asleep at last.

By the time Mum and Dad had a cup of tea and a chat it was nearly two o'clock when they went up to bed. Dad said to Mum, "One good thing about Bobby being so late in getting to sleep is that he will not waken up too early in the morning."

Well — it was only half-past four, and Mum and Dad were sound asleep, when Bobby burst into their bedroom and shouted, "He's been, he's been! Santa has been come and see the super things he has left for me!" So Mum and Dad tumbled out of bed and went through to inspect

Bobby's Christmas presents.

Among the things was a toy Santa Claus. Later in the day, Mum noticed this Santa Claus sitting on the floor all by itself while Bobby played with his other gifts. "Don't you like your Santa Claus?" asked Mum.

"Oh, yes," said Bobby, "it is nice."

"Have you seen what is inside it?" asked Mum.

"I didn't know there was anything inside it," answered Bobby. But when his toy Santa Claus was opened, Bobby found that it was full of chocolates.

Bobby thought his toy Santa Claus was nice; but he did not know just how nice it was, for he had not looked inside it.

Some people are like that about Christmas. They think it is nice but they do not realise just how nice it is, for they have not looked inside it. For Christmas is more than just parties and presents and Santa Claus. These things are just the 'outside' of Christmas. 'Inside', it is the birthday of Jesus.

Christmas is remembering that Jesus came to earth as a little child to be our Saviour and our Friend and that he wants us to find room in our hearts for him.

BOBBY LIKES THE TINSEL ON THE CHRISTMAS TREE

Bobby is very fond of Christmas. That is not surprising because most people like Christmas. And most people, too, are fond of Christmas trees. Bobby certainly is. There is always a lovely tree in Bobby's house at Christmas time. Bobby's church always has a lovely Christmas tree, too, with lots of fairy lights and other decorations.

Bobby was standing admiring the church Christmas tree one Sunday after morning service, when the minister came along. The minister said to Bobby, "It is a nice tree, isn't it, Bobby?"

"Yes, it is. It's beautiful," Bobby replied.

"What do you like best about it?" asked the minister, and he thought that Bobby was sure to say the fairy lights.

But Bobby gave him a surprise. Without any hesitation, he said "I like the tinsel best."

"Do you really?" said the minister, "why is that?"

"It's because of what it stands for," answered Bobby, "would you like me to tell you its story?"

"I certainly would," the minister said, "please do." And so Bobby told the minister the story of the tinsel, just as his Mum had told it to him.

"It was when Mary and Joseph and the baby Jesus were fleeing into Egypt," Bobby began. "The soldiers of Herod were pursuing them because they wanted to put to death every baby they could find. As Mary and Joseph hurried along with their baby, Mary became very tired and said that she would have to rest. Joseph knew that the soldiers might catch up with them if they took time to rest, but they had no choice because Mary was too tired to go on. And so they all went into a big dry cave to have a sleep.

"In that cave lived a spider and the spider knew that if the soldiers found the baby Jesus they would kill him because these were their orders from the cruel King Herod. 'I wish I could protect him' the spider said to herself, 'but I am too small and weak to be of much use'. Then she had an idea. 'I will do my best to hide the baby Jesus from the soldiers by spinning a web right across the mouth of the cave.'

"She began to spin and spin and spin as hard as ever she could. She kept spinning all through the night and by morning there was a huge spider's web covering the whole mouth of the cave in which the baby Jesus was sleeping.

"Just then Herod's soldiers arrived. They were looking everywhere for the baby Jesus to kill him, and were searching in all the caves they could see. But when they came to this particular cave, their captain saw the spider's web covering all its mouth and glistening like silver in the morning sun. 'We don't need to waste any time on this cave,' he said. 'Look at that giant spider's web. It's obvious that no one has gone in there for ages.'

"So the soldiers passed on and the baby Jesus' life was saved, all because a little spider did her best to help him. The tinsel on the Christmas tree stands for that spider's web, shining in the morning light."

When Bobby was finished, the minister said: "That's a

lovely story, Bobby. If you don't mind, I would like to tell it to the boys and girls next Sunday morning so that they will know that the tinsel on the Christmas tree reminds us that, no matter how small or weak we may be, doing our best for Jesus can be very important and helpful."

And that it just what he did.

Christmas Sunday

BOBBY AND THE FREE GIFT SHOP

One day when Bobby's mum took him shopping with her, they went into one shop which had a ticket on the counter beside a pile of little books, and the ticket said 'Please take one'. Bobby tugged at his mum's arm and asked, "What does that mean?"

"It means," said Mum, "that you can take one of those little books if you like. You don't need to pay anything for them."

So Bobby took one, but it was a disappointment. It was not a book of stories or pictures. It was just a book about the things you could buy in the shop.

Next they went to another shop whose window was full of lovely toys and games and inside there were more of them.

"Mum," whispered Bobby, "is this a 'Please take one' shop? Can I take one of the toys without paying anything for it?"

"I am afraid not, Bobby. You have to pay for anything you want in this shop."

So Bobby was disappointed again. But every morning after that he stopped and looked into the shop window, for it was on his way to school. He pressed his nose right up against the glass and wished he could take some of the lovely things home. But he never had any money.

One morning, however, when he pressed his nose up against the window it went right through. The glass was no longer there and right in the middle of all the toys and games was a notice that said, 'Please take one'. Bobby was so pleased and so excited. He could take anything he liked and it was free. How marvellous that was. He was so pleased and excited that he had to shout out, "Hurrah, hurrah".

And when he did, he woke himself up, for it was all a dream. What a disappointment that was!

"I should have known," said Bobby to himself, "that it was only a dream. There aren't any free gift shops like that in real life. You don't get good things for nothing."

Bobby was not altogether right, really. We *do* get some good things for nothing. In fact some of the best things in life are free.

We got our lives for free. God just gave them to us.

We did not have to buy our dads and mums. You did not have to go into a shop and say, "Please can I have a nice daddy—but he'll have to be cheap as I have not much money." Or go into another shop and say, "I see mummies are expensive today. When will there be a sale?"

Some very good things in this life come to us quite free. And the best thing of all is also a free gift. It is God's Christmas gift to every one of us, the gift of Jesus to be our Saviour and Friend.